I got more information in one reading [than] *I've received at any of the writers* [conferences] *in recent years. Mary clearly defines the* [...] *book and pulls it all together in easy to* [follow], [logical] *steps. I wish this book had been available before I wrote my first two novels.*

—D. Gordon Johnston, M.D.
Author, *Desert Winds* and *Lethal Mutation*

The god of good fortune, Ho Tai, brought me Mary Embree, Literary Consultant. If it were not for her, my book would not be in print. She guided me through the maze of editing, proof-reading, query letters, external and internal book design, publishing and agents—all issues that I found completely foreign and confusing.

—Thomas Quin Kong, M.D.
Author, *Tien Ming: Destiny*

I saw your fine hand in the well-crafted proposal. . . . As usual, you are to be commended for your professionalism.

—Richard F.X. O'Connor, Author and
Executive Editor, Renaissance Books

When I was writing my first magazine article, Mary Embree was a skilled guide to the nuts and bolts of the publishing process, from query letter to final submission.

—Mary Palevsky, Ph.D.
Author of *Atomic Fragments: A Daughter's Questions*

Mary Embree has been an inspiration to me in all of my writing. She has helped me make every sentence and paragraph come alive! It has been a joy to work with her.

—Martha K. Dane, Ph.D.
Author of books on spirituality

When Mary edits she shows you a direct path to accomplish a good rewrite. She has the answers to help make your work look great.

—Frances R. Riley
Author of children's books

Many thanks for your superb presentation on query letters. It was extremely well received by VCWC members and the many others who attended at Borders. I'm sure you were aware of the enthusiastic response and the many who wanted copies of your materials. What you had to say was very helpful to all of us who have to make contact with publishers and magazine editors and we all appreciated the valuable tips you provided.

—Gerald Schiller, Novelist
Past President of the Ventura County Writers Club

Your "Seven Vital Elements of a Successful Book Proposal" was one of the most useful and practical things I have ever encountered for writers concerned about communicating the scope and potential of their writing projects. Congrats on creating a really succinct and practical guide that made a difference in focusing and marketing my future writing projects.

—Stephen Rhodes, Novelist
The Betrayal Game and *The Velocity of Money*

The Apostolic Gospel (2 Corinthians 5:11–6:2)

Read the first two paragraphs of this section of the study to the group. In what sense is the gospel primarily about reconciliation? Reconciliation between what parties? Why?

The Apostolic Life (2 Corinthians 6:3-10)

Discuss these questions from the study: "How many of us would be so committed to the Lord that we would endure the hardships detailed by Paul in verses 3-10? And not only endure, but also see these hardships as badges of faithfulness, proving our trustworthiness as ministers of God's hope for reconciliation?"

Appeal for an Open Heart (2 Corinthians 6:11–7:4)

Read this section of the study to the group. Do you agree with its conclusion about the "key to reconciliation"?

The Joy of Reconciliation (2 Corinthians 7:5-16)

Titus has brought Paul word that at least some in the Corinthian congregation are eager for reconciliation. When have you been able to be a mediator or connecting link between two warring parties so that their relationship could be mended?

The Collection for Jerusalem (2 Corinthians 8:1–9:15)

The writer tells us that Paul may have viewed the offering he was soliciting for impoverished believers in Jerusalem as an opportunity for conciliation between Jewish and Gentile believers. Why do you think he said "conciliation" this time instead of "reconciliation"? What is the difference?

What is the financial stewardship principle embedded in Paul's discussion of the offering?

Live the Story

Invite participants to discuss the questions included in the "Live the Story" section of the study. Make sure to spend some time on the last block of questions. Those especially lead participants away from simply *talking about* reconciliation to actually acting to *initiate* reconciliation. Encourage any who identify someone from whom they are estranged to deal with the final question: "When will you do it?"

The
Author's Toolkit

A Step-by-Step Guide
to Writing a Book

Mary Embree

 Seaview Publishing

★Seaview Publishing
P.O. Box 2625
Ventura, CA 93002-2625

The Author's Toolkit
A Step-by-Step Guide to Writing a Book

Copyright © 2000 by Mary Embree

The discussion on contracts and any other legal matters is offered for general reference only. If legal advice is required, the services of a qualified attorney who is expert in the field of publishing law should be sought.

Cover design: Robert Aulicino

Library of Congress Control Number: 00-090614

Publisher's Cataloging-in-Publication
(Provided by Quality Books, Inc.)

Embree, Mary
    The author's toolkit : a step-by-step guide to writing a book / Mary Embree. — 1st ed.
    p. cm.
    LCCN: 00-90614
    ISBN: 0-9700682-0-4

    1. Authorship. 2. Authorship—Marketing
I. Title.

PN147.E43 2000   808'.02
                         QBI00-433

Printed in the United States of America

Acknowledgments

I want to thank the following people who helped, inspired, and encouraged me to write about writing.

My daughter Julie and son Joey, who as children taught me the three most important principles of writing: truth, clarity, and simplicity.

My mother, the great storyteller, who made fantasy seem real and brought magic into my life.

My aunts, Nelsie and Lucile, the wise and stalwart nonagenarians who I lean on for spiritual support.

My clients and students, those talented writers who entrust their creative works to me, share their thoughts and dreams with me, and teach me more about writing than I could ever teach them.

Patty Fry, the author of eight published books (and counting), whose enthusiasm and persistence are amazing.

Virginia Lawrence, the technical genius who listens kindly when I complain and tells me how to do things in a way I can understand.

Jim Lane, who gives me good advice, finds mistakes I overlook and tells me honestly what he thinks even when I wince.

Maurine Moore, who read the first draft of this book and made excellent suggestions.

Brian Henley, a gifted writer and budding novelist, who kept me in touch with the younger reader.

To all the people involved in Small Publishers, Artists & Writers Network (SPAWN) for their friendship, helpfulness, and the knowledge they so generously share.

Contents

Chapter Four

Chapter Five

Chapter Six

Chapter Seven

Chapter Eleven

Chapter Twelve

Resources

The Author's Toolkit

Introduction

Do you love to write? Do you **need** to write? Would **not** writing pose a serious threat to your emotional well-being? To your mental health? Would you write even if you thought you might not be able to sell your work? Even if no one ever read it?

If you answered yes to any of those questions, this book is for you. It will tell you what you need to know to complete your manuscript and contact the appropriate agent or publisher. If you answered no to all of the above, go no further. Give this guide to someone who is determined to write a book no matter what it takes. If you are not seriously committed to the process, you might as well find another interest, because writing is not easy and getting published is even harder.

There is no guarantee that you will get a publishing contract if you do everything that is recommended here. Many publishers have gone out of business or have merged with or sold out to larger publishers. The trend has been toward fewer publishers buying fewer manuscripts. Their inventory has been drastically reduced and most of them want a sure thing—or what they believe is a sure thing. A new, unproven writer is going to have to have something outstanding in some way before a publisher will respond with anything more than a form letter of rejection. That is the bad news.

The good news is that there have been some amazing success stories about first-time authors getting terrific publishing contracts and turning out bestsellers.

Any story worth telling, any lesson worth teaching and any idea worth expressing is worth writing about. And if you can tell, teach or explain well, you can write a book. So if you really, really want to write, what's stopping you?

Maybe it seems to be too daunting a task—so many words, so many pages—and you don't even know where to begin. You may worry about how to make your book interesting, how to organize it and put it together coherently. When you have completed the final draft, you may not have a clue as to how to find an agent to represent it or a company to publish it. If you feel that way, you are not alone. Many first-time authors feel overwhelmed at the beginning. Even though I had done a lot of writing before, when it came to writing a book, I had all of those fearful feelings—until I learned the process.

Both editing and writing require large doses of concentration, discipline, passion, dedication, and integrity. Although writing can be enormously gratifying, good writing isn't easy, at least not for me or any of the other writers I know. Editing requires great attention to detail. There are some common pitfalls that I have noticed through working with nearly 100 writers during the past decade. I will explain how to avoid them and I'll give you some valuable principles you can apply both to your writing and editing.

I have worked with writers as a consultant, editor, cheerleader, and sounding board. Although I have been called a book doctor, I would prefer to be considered a teacher. Amos Bronson Alcott, educator, philosopher and the father of Louisa May Alcott, said, "The true teacher defends his pupils against his own personal influence. He inspires self-trust. He guides their eyes from himself to the spirit that quickens him. He will have no disciple."

My best teachers, when it came to expressing my thoughts and feelings, have been my children. From the time they were very young I read my poetry and song lyrics to them and asked them to tell me what they thought about them. They had definite opinions about what they liked and what they didn't. And they were very honest, as children usually are. They told me when they thought something I had written was corny or old-fashioned. They let me know when they didn't understand what I meant. Whenever I read something that was off the mark or that they thought was boring, it wasn't just what they said that told me I'd better do a rewrite, it was the looks on their faces. My children taught me how to write with more clarity and with fewer pretensions. I listened to them and I changed my writing accordingly. Oh, and by the way, they both grew up to become professional writers themselves.

The approach I use in this book is unconventional. Maybe that's because I've spent so much time around writers of all kinds. For a number of years I worked in television production in positions ranging from assistant to the producer and script reader to researcher and writer. I worked on a number of top-rated sitcoms (situation comedies). When I didn't have to be in the booth with the producer, I sat with the comedy writers as they watched the shows they had written being taped. They were not allowed in the studio because they were a rather unruly bunch so they watched the show on a TV monitor in a small room offstage. When they didn't like the way the actors read their lines, they'd throw banana peels and apple cores at the TV screen. During those years of working with entertainment writers and producers, I learned timing, pacing, continuity, plot constructions, and got an idea of what was funny and what was not. That was where I began to understand what a "hook" is. Even those successful, highly-paid writers didn't score on every play, I discovered. Although you can learn certain techniques, writing isn't a science. It's a creative endeavor.

When I decided to become a writer by profession, I began writing just about anything I could get paid for. That included educational audio- and videotape scripts, magazine articles, and television documentaries, pilots, treatments, and commercials. My last job in the television industry was in the mid-1980s when I worked as researcher and writer for *This is Your Life,* a series that had been popular in prior years which they were trying to revive. It lasted only one season, however, and by that time I was ready to get away from Hollywood and into a different field of writing.

In the early 1990s I did some editing and ghostwriting for doctors and scientists who wanted to reach a general audience and needed someone to put their ideas into layperson's language. My ignorance of their field was just what they needed. If I could understand what they were saying, I could explain it to others. In the mid-90s I wrote my first book under my own name and was fortunate enough to get an agent who found a publisher for it.

Through the years certain challenges have come up again and again. I began writing booklets on how to write query letters and prepare book proposals. I used them when I conducted workshops and seminars and the participants' questions and suggestions helped me put together this book.

In this guide you'll be taken through the detailed process, step-by-step, of turning your concept into a book of professional quality. You'll be shown some shortcuts to self-editing that could save you money on a proofreader and editor. You'll find out how to avoid some common traps that lie in wait for unsuspecting writers. You'll learn the format for presenting your proposed book to an agent or publisher.

Become familiar with the process and learn the rules. Then have the courage to break a few of those rules when they get in the way of what you want to say. My goal is to get you to trust your instincts, find your true voice, and let your creative passions run free.

—Mary Embree

Chapter One

IN THE BEGINNING IS THE IDEA

Ideas are to literature what light is to painting.

—Paul Bourget

*T*he Idea always comes first. You have to know what you want to write about before you start writing. Next comes the title. Or several possible titles. The title isn't important in the beginning because as you go along you may change it; you may find a title you hadn't thought of until you had written most of the book.

The concept sometimes changes. It may grow, improve, maybe even move in a different direction from that which you had originally planned. That's okay—if it works. If it goes off on a tangent, veers off the track, or becomes a different book, stop and take stock.

Reread what you have written. Do you really want to write a different book? If not, where did your writing start to go astray? You will find out quickly if you read it aloud to yourself. You will start to stumble over the words and you will know. Pull out what doesn't belong but don't throw it away. There may be some useful ideas there. Put those away for now. Then go back and pick up the thread of your story and start writing again.

Was it hard to get started? Is it tough to get going again? Kristen Hunter is quoted in *Black Women Writers at Work:* "Writing is harder than anything else; at least *starting* to write is."

Don't worry if you can't figure out what that first page, first paragraph, first sentence should be. You don't have to know that now. You might find after you have written 15 chapters that your book really starts at Chapter Five and you can throw away Chapters One, Two, Three, and Four or plug them in somewhere else.

I advise the nonfiction authors I work with to become familiar with the book proposal format or even to prepare a proposal as soon as the idea for a book occurs to them. There's probably nothing more disappointing to an author than to write a whole manuscript and find it doesn't have a chance of getting published. The research that must be done to write a proposal would turn up that information. Another reason to study the book proposal format is to help you organize your work.

PLAN YOUR BOOK

Do an outline or write chapter headings and a short paragraph on what's in each chapter. Some writers put this information on small index cards and arrange them on a table. They can then see the whole book at a glance and rearrange the cards if necessary. If you are writing a novel, write character sketches too. Get to know the information, people, and events that are involved in your story so that you can confidently introduce them to the reader. Once you have a plan, a road map of where you are going, you will never encounter writer's block.

Have a clear idea of what you want to say and then develop your concept along those lines. But don't be rigid. Let it flow like water in a stream, following its own natural course. Unleash your creativity; you can always cut and edit later. Make it interesting. If it interests you, it probably will interest others.

WRITE A ONE-SENTENCE DESCRIPTION

To help you focus on your subject, write one sentence that describes your book. Here are some examples from various bestseller lists. (F is for fiction; NF is for nonfiction.)

From Washington Post *Book World* (Bestsellers)

I Know This Much is True, by Wally Lamb. [F] *A man's complicated relationship with his schizophrenic brother.*

Single & Single, by John le Carre. [F] *The lives of a rogue English banker and a Russian mobster collide.*

Bittersweet, by Danielle Steel. [F] *A picture-perfect suburban housewife reconsiders her choices.*

From New York Times *Book Review* (Best Sellers)

The Girl Who Loved Tom Gordon, by Stephen King. [F] *When a young girl gets lost in the woods, she is saved by her spiritual association with a relief pitcher for the Boston Red*

Sox.

The Greatest Generation, by Tom Brokaw. [NF] *The lives of men and women who came of age during the Depression and World War II.*

I **Thee Wed,** by Amanda Quick. [F] *After finding a job as a lady's maid on an English estate, a woman discovers surprising challenges and romance.*

From Los Angeles Times *Book Review* (Bestsellers)

The Ground Beneath Her Feet, by Salman Rushdie. [F] *Orpheus and Eurydice are a couple of modern day rock'n'roll stars.*

Another Country, by Mary Pipher. [NF] *Old age and its myriad concerns, financial, physical and emotional, and a criticism of our youth-obsessed culture.*

Blues for All the Changes, by Nikki Giovanni. [F] *Fifty-two intensely personal new poems on sex and politics and love "among Black folk."*

Here's what all three lists say about **The Poisonwood Bible,** by Barbara Kingsolver [F]

A missionary family's life in the Congo over the course of 30 years. [Washington Post]

Five female characters narrate this novel set in the Belgian Congo. [New York Times]

An evangelical Baptist missionary takes his wife and children to the Belgian Congo in 1959. [Los Angeles Times]

📖 📖 📖

As you can see, there isn't any one way to explain what a

book is about. But the above will give you an idea of how you could describe yours. There will be more about this in the chapters on Query Letters and Book Proposals.

By the way, how sharp is your eye? Did you notice that the *New York Times* calls them "Best Sellers" while the *Washington Post* and the *Los Angeles Times* list them as "Bestsellers"? Which is correct: best sellers or bestsellers? They both are. See the chapter on Editing Principles regarding styles and consistency.

For most of us who possess the soul of a writer, there are book ideas that call us, begging us to write them and bring them out of obscurity. I think it would be sad to reach the end of our days and lie on our deathbed regretting that we never did write that book—the one that tugged at our heart for so many years.

What is the book that calls to you? Is it nonfiction? Are there valuable lessons you could teach? Is there important information you could share? Is it a family history or an autobiography that generations of relatives who come after you would treasure? Is it a novel that is trying to get your attention? Deep inside you, are there voices that long to be heard; voices that only you can unsilence? Are there fascinating characters only you can bring to life? Will you let them languish mutely within the prison of your mind or turn them loose upon the world to tell their story?

📖 📖 📖

When you take it one word at a time, it isn't so intimidating. And, after all, that is the only way you *can* write it. Here is an exercise to get you started:

➢ Choose several possible titles for your book.

➢ Check *Books in Print, Forthcoming Books,* or an Internet bookstore such as Amazon.com to see if the titles you've chosen have been used. (See Chapter Two, Researching)

➤ Write a few one-sentence descriptions that tell succinctly what your book is about.

Chapter Two

RESEARCHING

When you steal from one author, it's plagiarism;
if you steal from many, it's research.

—Wilson Mizner

No matter what you are writing about, the likelihood is that you will need to do some research on the subject. If you are writing nonfiction, research is essential. No matter how well you know your subject, your memory isn't perfect and even if it were there are changes that take place all the time that may make your knowledge outdated. You will have to be sure that your information is accurate, current, and has not already been written about in the way you intend to write it.

Even if you are writing a novel there is likely to be information you will need. For example, suppose your protagonist is a cardiologist. You will need to know something about heart problems, surgical procedures, hospital protocol, and so forth. If the action in your novel takes place in Hong Kong you will have to know enough about the geography, climate, customs, people, and laws to make your story feel authentic. It helps if you've been to Hong Kong but if you haven't been there recently and your story is set in the present time, you'll need to find out what it's like there now. There have been a lot of political changes in Hong Kong in the past few years.

You must be accurate about dates, the spelling of names, historical events, recent developments in your subject field, and on and on. The list is endless. The integrity of your research can make you look expert or amateurish.

Where do you find all this information? Fortunately for writers, the information highway has been repaved and many more lanes have been added. Here are the major ways to find the data you need.

THE INTERNET

Where we once had to get out of our house or office and go to the library, we can now get just about any information we need over the Internet. There is a caveat, however, to getting your facts that way. Not all of the information is unbiased and accurate. You will still have to be sure of your sources. And there isn't a friendly librarian sitting inside your computer who will help you through the maze of Web sites and tell you what to click on. You still have to know exactly what you are looking for and where to find it.

THE LIBRARY

You could call the librarian of your local library and ask her to locate, copy, and send the information you are seeking to you. Libraries are so understaffed now, though, that services such as that may no longer be available. You might have to go to the library to look things up yourself. But sometimes it's very nice—and inspiring—to get out of your office or house and go sit among the books.

The librarian will teach you how to use the card file and their own computers to locate where in the library you will find what you need, if you don't already know how to do so. They may have reference books in the library that you can't get on the Internet. For instance, *Literary Market Place* (LMP) has a Web site but, if you are not a paid subscriber, only a small portion of the information that is in their huge annual reference book is available to you on their Web site. The printed issues of the books and the online subscription are both very expensive.

Usually you can access R.R. Bowker's *Books in Print* and *Forthcoming Books* on the library's computer. When you start doing research for your book proposal, these lists and LMP will be essential.

ENCYCLOPEDIAS

If you have the printed edition of the *Encyclopedia Brittanica* and it is recent, that's great. It is still considered by most experts to be the best encyclopedia. If not, you can get it and other encyclopedias on CDs which are considerably less costly than the printed versions. Again, it is essential to have a recently published encyclopedia. The information you need may not be in an older issue or may be out of date.

DICTIONARIES

It is imperative for a writer to have an unabridged dictionary in addition to a desk dictionary. I recommend *Webster's Third New International Dictionary* and *Webster's New*

Collegiate Dictionary. Webster's New Universal Unabridged Dictionary is also good. There is more on this subject in the chapter on editing. Again, make sure you have a recent edition. Technology is changing so fast that dictionaries are out of date even before they are published. The 1991 edition of *Webster's New Collegiate Dictionary* doesn't have the words *Internet* or *Web site* in it. Neither does the 1996 unabridged dictionary.

ALMANACS

There's a wealth of information of all sorts in *The World Almanac, The Information Please Almanac* and other books of this kind. As an example of the kind of information you may find in an almanac, a recent edition of *The World Almanac and Book of Facts* contained an article on the transition of power in Hong Kong when China regained control after 156 years of British rule. Since almanacs come out with new editions every year, they will have more recent information than some encyclopedias.

Another reference book of this type is *The Cambridge Factfinder* published by Cambridge University Press. It contains a "collection of bits of information for use in the home, at school, or in the office" and claims to contain more facts than any other book of its kind. A fact is not a single, isolated piece of information, according to the publisher, and "A factbook is not intended to do the job of a glossary, a manual, or a textbook."

The Oxford English Dictionary defines a fact as "Something that has really occurred or is actually the case; something certainly known to be of this character; hence a particular truth known by actual observation or authentic testimony, as opposed to what is merely inferred, or to a conjecture or fiction; a datum of experience, as opposed to the conclusions which may be based upon it."

Defining what a fact actually is proves to be elusive because there are facts about fictions and fictions about facts. It is often hard to determine what is fact and what is fiction. *The Cambridge Factfinder* states that "There are near-facts (estimates of X), transient facts (world records about X), qualified facts (the majority of X), arguable facts (the most important X), politically biased facts (the growth or decline of X), and contrived facts (neat classifications of X)."

Even so, if you are ever called to explain how you got your information, it's comforting to be able to cite a source to show that you didn't make up your facts.

REFERENCE BOOKS SPECIFIC TO YOUR SUBJECT

If you write regularly on historical subjects, medicine, alternative health, animals, or whatever, it's a good idea to accumulate reference books on these subjects. For example, if you were writing articles or a book having to do with health, you might need a medical dictionary, a family medical guide, or books on nutrition, pharmaceuticals, herbal medicines, and various forms of natural healing.

NEWSPAPERS AND MAGAZINES

Keep up with what is happening in the world on a daily basis. Subscribe to a newspaper, preferably a major one such as the *Washington Post,* the *Wall Street Journal,* the *New York Times,* or the *Los Angeles Times.* They may not, however, be unbiased in their reporting. Also subscribe to magazines and journals in your field. They will have more current information than other sources but they may contain organizational bias.

ORGANIZATIONS

Join organizations that are formed to put people together with similar interests and attend their meetings. There is no way to over-emphasize the importance of networking with people in the field you are writing about. They are a valuable source of information, inspiration and assistance.

EXPERTS AND OTHER AUTHORS

When you need expert advice, go to someone who knows the field and subject well. It could take you hours to get the answer to a question through other forms of research when you might be able to contact experts who will answer your question in a matter of minutes. Most of the time this can be done on the phone and you can record the conversation (with their permission).

Reference books should be kept in your home or office library and replaced each time a new edition comes out. Having information at your fingertips when you need it can be a real time-saver.

Researching can be very time-consuming when most of us would really rather be writing, but it can make the difference between producing an authoritative, informed, and interesting book and one that is merely mediocre.

Chapter Three

THE RULES OF WRITING

"Fool!" said my muse to me,
"look in thy heart, and write."

—Sir Philip Sidney,
Astrophel and Stella [1591]

Think of your proposed book as a story. No matter what you are writing—a how-to or self-help book, an autobiography or a novel—you should have a story in mind: a beginning, a middle, and an end. There must be a basic concept, continuity, and logical transitions from one paragraph to the next and one chapter to the next.

How do you begin? If you don't have a plan, just start writing and write until you have a clear idea of what your book is about. Don't stop and edit the first two pages again and again before you go on. Keep writing until you get your first draft down. Some writers do an outline before they begin and that's usually a good idea. But your initial outline can be brief, just chapter titles with a few words about what will be included in each one.

What writing implement should you use? Whatever feels most comfortable. A woman writer I know who was a touch-typist and could type fast still wrote all of her first drafts in longhand. She said, "I can be more creative when I can feel my ideas flow from my brain, down my arm and through my fingers, pour into the pencil and spread onto the paper."

Many writers still write their first draft that way. Another writer told me he wrote with a pencil so that he could erase and make corrections. Soon he realized that he was erasing stuff that was better than his "corrections." After that he drew a line through the words he was replacing. Later, he began to write incomplete sentences longhand just to get his ideas down on paper quickly and then fleshed them out when he typed them up. When he graduated from his old IBM Selectric to the computer, he discovered he could compose right at the keyboard with no loss of creativity. Now he almost never writes anything in longhand. He says that he can type much faster than he writes. "I can get my thoughts down on paper before they fly away and settle upon the next idea."

Which is the best way to write? Whichever way works best for you.

If you like to think out loud, you may be more comfortable talking into a tape recorder and having someone transcribe it for you. Now you can even dictate your book directly to disk on your computer with speech recognition software. Then you can print your first draft and start editing and refining it.

WRITE FROM THE HEART

Whatever you are writing, be enthusiastic about your subject. Whether it is a mystery novel or a how-to book it must stir your passion or you will have trouble making it interesting. If you write a book simply because you think that it will sell, the process itself will not be rewarding and you will probably end up with a dry, dull book.

In his book, *On Writing Well*, William Zinsser states, "Ultimately the product that any writer has to sell is not the subject being written about, but who he or she is." Your zeal, integrity, and warmth will draw a reader into your book, not hard facts and cold statistics.

In *The Metamorphosis*, Franz Kafka wrote, "As Gregor Samsa awoke one morning from uneasy dreams he found himself transformed in his bed into a gigantic insect."

"When I read the line," Gabriel Garcia Marquez, author of *One Hundred Years of Solitude,* is quoted as saying, "I thought to myself I didn't know anyone was allowed to write things like that. If I had known, I would have started writing a long time ago. So I immediately started writing short stories."

IF YOU WOULD WRITE, READ

Read works that inspire you, excite you, enlighten or surprise you—books that touch your feelings. Read books that are quoted often like the Bible, and the works of Shakespeare and John Donne. Read the classics, the current bestsellers, and any books that may be a lot like the one you are writing. In *The Writing Life*, author Annie Dillard said, "[The writer] is careful of what he reads, for that is what he will write."

KEEP IT SIMPLE

In 1580 Michel Eyquem de Montaigne wrote, "I want to be seen here in my simple, natural, ordinary fashion, without straining or artifice; for it is myself that I portray. . . . I am myself the matter of my book."

The most powerful writing is that which flows naturally and simply, expressing the thoughts and feelings of the author in a clear, direct, and honest way. Leo Nikolaevich Tolstoi said that "there is no greatness where there is not simplicity, goodness and truth."

Long, complex sentences tend to be confusing and murky. Don't put more than one or two ideas into a sentence. Get rid of the clutter in your writing as you would your old, outdated clothes. Clean out the closet of your mind and let the sunlight and fresh air in.

I've learned a great deal about my own writing through editing other writers. It's so much easier to see other people's mistakes. We get used to our own and either don't recognize them as mistakes or become protective of them.

WHEN IN DOUBT, TAKE IT OUT!

One of the best secrets of good writing I ever learned I discovered quite by accident while I was editing a nonfiction book by a medical doctor. I kept coming across complicated sentences and couldn't figure out what the author meant. As he tried to explain them to me I realized that he had already stated the ideas earlier in his manuscript and in a much clearer way. In his efforts to reiterate what he thought was important, he had made his work more confusing. I found that it wasn't a matter of rewriting the lines to make them understandable. We could take the sentence out entirely without losing anything. His points then became more discernible and the writing flowed more gracefully.

You can't write clearly unless you are sure about what you want to say. I applied my new rule of "when in doubt, take it out" to other clients' works—as well as to my own—and the results were amazing.

KEEP YOUR WRITING CLEAN AND CLEAR

Strip it of words and phrases that serve no function or are redundant. "The art of the writer," Ralph Waldo Emerson said, "is to speak his fact and have done. Let the reader find that he cannot afford to omit any line of your writing, because you have omitted every word that he can spare."

Replace multi-syllabic words with words of one or two syllables. Walt Whitman wrote, "The art of art, the glory of expression and the sunshine of the light of letters, is simplicity." Complicated sentences that are difficult to read and understand will turn away a reader. Let lawyers and lawmakers write like that; it isn't for those of us who want to write books people will want to read.

SHOW, DON'T TELL

What does that mean? I recently had an e-mail conversation with Jim Lane, a friend of mine and a successful writer whose work I admire mightily. He wrote that he had been listening to an author interview on National Public Radio. The author had asserted that "a novel is ALL telling—that is what a story is."

Jim's reaction, "barring purely semantic differences," was to agree. "Usually we try to 'show' through dialog because everything else is, by necessity, telling. Yet we would be hard-pressed to tell a story in dialog alone. And sometimes telling—simple, declarative statements—is the most efficient way to advance the story. As with so many other rules [show, don't tell] has become simplified to the point of being wrong.

"We may be able to reveal some facets of character through dialog but not the whole character," Jim continued. "There are things a character wouldn't say or even intimate, perhaps not even think.

"Maybe a better rule (goal) for we novelists is to consider dialog and exposition in the light of maintaining pace. Maybe the next time someone exhorts that we show don't tell, we ask for an explanation of exactly how to do it efficiently, without ruining flow and pace. And, what's wrong with telling if we do it in a lively, colorful way?"

There is absolutely nothing wrong with telling when it is done in an interesting way, I agreed. It is easier though, I believe, to make our words come to life when we show rather than tell. What exactly is meant by showing when we are only using words? A manuscript I recently edited made one area of showing, not telling, clear to me. The author frequently interrupted the narration to tell what the characters were thinking. He believed it was important to explain their motivations and feelings. However, it broke the momentum of the exciting story he had written and it distracted me so much that I took most of the "thinking" out.

When the author read my edited draft, he did not object to the cuts. As it was a mystery novel he was writing, getting rid of those digressions kept the story zipping along at a rapid pace and kept the reader involved. In this particular book, it wasn't important to know what the character was feeling. The author had defined the personalities of his characters very well as he introduced each one. After that it was, in fact, more interesting to speculate about the character's thoughts and motivations.

A character can show what he is thinking by what he does. Using words to describe actions rather than thoughts usually works better.

Instead of writing that John was startled when Marsha came up behind him, you could explain what your characters did. *When Marsha crept up quietly behind John and tapped him on the shoulder, he jumped as though he had been struck.*

Here's another example. Rather than *It made her nervous when he looked at her,* you could write, *When his eyes locked upon hers, she quickly looked away and started fidgeting with her napkin.*

Telling is: *She was bored.*

Showing is: *She yawned and stared blankly out the window.*

You could say that a character was angry or hurt or amused but it's more visual if you describe what a character did to show those feelings.

Showing can also be done through dialog very effectively. Eve could say, *"I'm so bored I could scream. There's not even anything on TV."* And instead of saying that Adam was hurt by her indifference to him, you could write that *Adam's shoulders sagged and his eyes got cloudy as he replied, "But I thought you'd enjoy spending the evening sitting here with me by a cozy fire."*

There are times to use the passive voice and times to use the active voice. Among Webster's definitions of *passive* are:

> *adj.* not reacting visibly to something that might be expected to produce manifestations of an emotion or feeling . . . of, pertaining to, or being a voice, verb form, or construction having a subject represented as undergoing the action expressed by the verb, as the sentence *The letter was written last week* (opposed to active).

Webster's defines *active* as:

adj. engaged in action or activity; characterized by energetic work, motion, etc. . . . of, pertaining to, or being a voice, verb form, or construction having a subject represented as performing or causing the action expressed by the verb, as the verb form *write* in *I write letters every day* (opposed to passive).

When presented with a choice of passive or active writing, try action first, dialog second and everything else after that. To show is to write more externally, more expressively. But, I agree with Jim that there are times when telling (using the passive voice) moves a story along best. As writers, we are faced with decisions with every word we write.

AVOID CLICHÉS

What is a **cliché?** Webster defines it as

n. 1. a trite, stereotyped expression, as *sadder but wiser,* or *as strong as an ox.* 2. (in art, literature, drama, etc.) a trite or hackneyed plot, character development, use of form, musical style, etc. 3. anything that has become trite or commonplace through overuse.

Lazy writers use clichés. Creative writers avoid them. If an expression comes easily, question it. In *A Dictionary of Modern English Usage [1926]* Francis George Fowler wrote that when the use of hackneyed phrases come into the writer's mind they should be viewed as danger signals. "He should take warning that when they suggest themselves it is because what he is writing is bad stuff, or it would not need such help; let him see to the substance of his cake instead of decorating with sugarplums."

There was recently a politician who was so wont to use clichés that he was frequently quoted even though (or maybe because) there was very little substance in what he had to say. Here are a few that I found in one short speech he made:

"I think this thing is a *rush to judgment.*"

"We would not *sweep it under the rug.*"

"If you think you're going to win this on what public opinion polls say 18 months out, *I beg to differ.*"

"He's going to be in for *a rude awakening.*"

Who is that cliché-addicted politician? As he might be one of your heroes, I'm not going to say. When it turned out the man was not going to run for president after all, the newspaper journalists were disappointed—he was such a rich source of trite expressions.

Although it is rare, occasionally there is a place for clichés. Vladimir Nabakov, in talking about his book *Lolita* said, "In pornographic novels, action has to be limited to the copulation of clichés. Style, structure, imagery should never distract the reader from his tepid lust."

The caveat is: think carefully before you use a familiar phrase. Is there a reason for it? Does it define a character? Does it fit so well that any other expression would not do? If the answer to these questions is no, then try to express the same idea in an entirely new way.

AVOID SLANG

Unless it is dialog peculiar to a character, or illustrates the era, or has a definite use in your particular work, do not use slang. Slang words and expressions are in a constant state of flux, slipping in and out of style in short spans of time. Therefore, using slang will date you or your book.

Hip, defined as "familiar with the latest ideas, styles, developments, etc.; up-to-date; with-it," was once *hep* as in *hep cat.* These words probably originated with musicians.

Neat, cool, hot, bitchin', bad, righteous, fly, and *dope* are all words that mean very good-looking, exciting, sexy or anything really terrific. *Phat* is a word meaning roughly the same thing. Depending on who I asked, I heard that it means pretty, hot and tempting, or something or someone extraordinarily appealing. *Extra large* means really *phat.*

A word that is acceptable in one culture may not be in another. Musicians may use one term while computer programmers use another to express the same idea. Slang will be different from one ethnic group and one region to another. Many of the slang expressions that have now become part of our language originated with avant garde musicians of various eras, such as the pioneers of jazz, rock and hip-hop. New language creators are often young people living in poor neighborhoods.

The use of profanity has changed, too. Swear words are used more widely than ever before by the general public. In many environments, such as the entertainment business, there are no longer any forbidden words. Anything goes. We hear a lot of swear words on the playground and in schools now, as children have incorporated them into their daily language. I don't wish to discuss the right or wrong of such a development but simply to call attention to the changing mores of language. But, morality aside, the use of profanity, like clichés, often shows a distinct lack of creativity.

In a novel, the use of slang, profanity, and ethnic expressions can be instrumental in showing the identity or nature of a character. It can add color and authenticity. In nonfiction writing, however, unless the book is about slang or profanity, it's usually best to avoid it.

There are as many different ways to write as there are writers. Still, if you're going to do a thing, do it well. Don't take the easy way out. In accepting the Nobel Prize, Ernest

Hemingway said, "For a true writer each book should be a new beginning where he tries again for something that is beyond attainment."

Chapter Four

EDITING PRINCIPLES

*I can't write five words but
that I change seven.*

—Dorothy Parker

With computers, more writers are able to produce works on their own. That means publishers are getting an avalanche of manuscripts. With competition stiffer than ever, books needing extensive editing are often rejected. As many publishers don't have the staff they once had, their decision about whether to publish your book may depend on how much work needs to be done on it. When they find a book they like that has also been well edited, they are more likely to take it on.

Many writers are now hiring professional editors to put

the final polish on their manuscripts before they send them off. But that can be costly so it's best to edit as much as you can first. In addition to the obvious—incorrect spelling and grammar—here are some other things to look out for.

➤ uncommon words repeated in a sentence

➤ repetitions of all kinds: phrases, ideas, descriptions

➤ long, complex sentences and choppy sentences

➤ inconsistencies in style and punctuation

RECOMMENDED REFERENCE BOOKS

If you have no other reference books, it is essential that you have a dictionary and a style book and check them often. There are several books on style but most book publishers recommend *The Chicago Manual of Style*. Styles of writing and word usage change constantly so it's best to get the latest issue. The most recent one was published in 1993 and it is almost 200 pages longer than the prior 1982 issue.

The *Manual* is considered by many to be essential for all writers, editors, proofreaders, copywriters, publishers and anyone else who works with words. Although the publisher states that it's easier to use than ever before, it takes some getting used to. It is still hard to find just what you're looking for until you become familiar with the way the book is laid out. The *Manual* contains a wealth of information on many subjects. In addition to word usage, abbreviations, titles, forms of address, punctuation and all of those details, it also covers manuscript preparation, rights and permissions and many other subjects.

Since the advent of the computer, styles have changed. One example is that instead of spacing twice after a period and before the next sentence, we now space only once. When we typed on a typewriter, we used to underline book titles; now we italicize them. I will cover some of the more common questions I get from writers but it's not possible to address all the issues here. You will need a style book.

For spelling, the *Chicago Manual of Style* recommends *Webster's Third New International Dictionary* and its abridged *Webster's New Collegiate Dictionary*. *Webster's New Universal Unabridged Dictionary* (based on the Second Edition of the Random House *Dictionary of the English Language)* is also considered outstanding. Washington Post Book World calls it "without a doubt, today's unabridged dictionary of choice." The most recent edition is 1996.

For more casual use, there is the Random House *Webster's College Dictionary*. Unlike the unabridged, it's small enough to fit on a desk. Whichever dictionary you choose, use the same one throughout the editing of each manuscript so that you will be consistent. When two spellings of a word are given, use the first listed because it is the preferred spelling.

The Professional Looking Manuscript

Think of your writing as your baby. Creating and birthing it isn't enough. It needs nurturing and changing to become the best it can be. Good enough isn't good enough. It's got to be better than anything else out there to even get noticed.

Whether you are getting your manuscript and/or book proposal ready to send to an agent, a publisher, or a book doctor/editor, self-editing is an important part of your writing. The following are some things to look for.

Format

Although we are dealing primarily with manuscripts for

books here, these principles apply to all kinds of writing. Present your work in the standard format for that genre.

For example: query letters and synopses for a proposed book are single-spaced; the other parts of the book proposal, the sample chapters and the pages of your manuscript are double-spaced. There is a special format for television scripts for a half-hour taped series, a different format for a TV script for a "movie of the week" or a miniseries, and still a different format for theatrical film scripts.

Do your research, get samples of these formats if you can, and pattern your presentation according to the standards of the industry, genre and entity to which you are making your presentation.

ACCURACY

Always check spelling and word usage. Is it one word, a hyphenated word, or two words? For instance, you might say "this is for your *eyes only*" but "this is an *eyes-only* report." Both *crows-nest* and *crows nest* are acceptable but not *crowsnest*. Different dictionaries may have different spellings for the same word. Sometimes it takes a few years for a new word to settle down to one preferred spelling.

There are words that you may not find in any dictionary that's less than five or ten years old. If you can't find a dictionary that contains newly coined words such as *Internet* and *Web site*, check several sources, such as newspapers, magazines, and computer manuals for these words. But even that may not help you. I've seen *Web site* spelled *web site,* and *website*. When in doubt choose one and stick to it throughout your manuscript. The main thing, again, is to be consistent.

Your computer's spell-check is helpful but has its limitations. Beware of errors it will not pick up, such as using *their* (possessive case of they) when it should be *there* (in or at that place) and *emigrate* (to leave a country to live elsewhere) when you mean *immigrate* (to enter a country to live there). Here are some words that are often used incorrectly:

accept	to receive; to answer affirmatively
except	to leave out, with the exclusion of
advice	an opinion or recommendation
advise	to give counsel to
affect	to influence, to pretend
effect	a result, an influence, an impression
appraise	to determine the worth of
apprise	to give notice of; inform; acquaint
auger	a tool
augur	a prophet (noun); to prophesy (verb)
born	brought forth by birth
borne	past participle of the verb bear: to support
brake	to reduce speed; a retarding device
break	to separate; to destroy; to fracture
canvas	cloth; picture
canvass	to examine or seek opinions
capital	a seat of government; money
Capitol	the building in Washington D.C. where Congress holds its sessions
compare	to liken; to relate
contrast	to examine differences
continual	intermittent; often repeated
continuous	uninterrupted in time

councilor	member of a council
counselor	one who gives advice
complement	something that completes
compliment	an expression of admiration
criminologist	one who studies crime
criminalist	a forensic investigator
disburse	to pay out; to spend
disperse	to scatter; to dissipate; to spray
energize	to give energy to
enervate	to destroy the vigor of; weaken
flair	skill, talent; aptitude
flare	a bright light, an outburst
flaunt	to show off; display ostentatiously
flout	to show contempt for; scoff at
forbear	to refrain or abstain from; to forgo
forebear	ancestor; forefather; progenitor
forego	to go before; to precede
forgo	to give up; to renounce
foreword	introduction in a book; a preface
forward	toward or to what is in front of
gibe	to jeer or taunt
jibe	to be in agreement or to shift sails
gorilla	an ape
guerrilla	a member of a military force
hail	to acclaim; to attract: *hail a cab*
hale	healthy, robust, vigorous
hoard	a stash (noun); to store away (verb)
horde	a wandering group or a swarm

illegible	impossible or hard to read
unreadable	not interesting; not worth reading
imply	to indicate
infer	to draw a conclusion
ingenious	brilliant, clever
ingenuous	simple, naive
its	belonging to it
it's	it is
lay	to set down; also past tense of **lie**
lie	to rest in a horizontal position; to make an untrue statement
liable	responsible; likely
libel	a defamatory statement
mantel	facing of a fireplace; a shelf above
mantle	a cloak; something that conceals
notable	worthy, impressive
notorious	widely known and *ill-regarded*
prescribe	appoint; to order a medicine
proscribe	to prohibit; to banish or exile
principal	main, foremost (adjective); the person in charge (noun)
principle	a moral rule; a law
rack	framework; spread out; torture
wrack	damage or destruction
retch	to make efforts to vomit
wretch	an unfortunate or unhappy person
than	used after comparative words such as other (conjunction)

then	at that time; immediately or soon afterward; next in order (adverb)
whose	possessive case of which or who
who's	who is
your	belonging to you
you're	you are

Here are some examples of word misusage that are seen often: "very unique" and "as perfect as it gets." *Unique* and *perfect* are absolutes, like *complete, equal, dead* and *pregnant.* You can't be a little or a lot of any of those; you either are or you aren't. Unique means existing as the only one or as the sole example. Perfect describes an absolute condition that cannot exist in degrees. You could say "almost perfect" or "as close to perfect as it gets."

Okay, I'll admit that when I looked *unique* and *perfect* up in the dictionary, I saw that they have undergone semantic development and that the careless usage I pointed out above has become standard in all varieties of speech and writing. Even the writers of the U.S. Constitution said, "in order to form a more perfect union." But I still think it's wrong to qualify those words and whenever I see it done on a manuscript, I circle it in red. There are no other *unqualified* words that can take their place.

Other words frequently misused are "that" when it should be "who" as in "Is she the woman *that* sold you the hat?" instead of "Is she the woman *who* sold you the hat?" A person is a who; a thing is a that.

Was is sometimes used in the subjunctive mood when the appropriate word is *were.* Subjunctive is a grammatical mood typically used for doubtful or hypothetical statements. For example, one would say <u>*when* I *was* young</u> but <u>*if* I *were* young.</u>

The word "whom" has gone almost completely out of style. And good riddance. Most people use it incorrectly anyway. I quote directly from *Random House Webster's College Dictionary:*

> By the strict rules of grammar, "who" is the correct form for the subject of a sentence or clause *(Who said that? The guard who let us in checked our badges),* and "whom" is used for the object of a verb or preposition *(Whom did you ask? To whom are we obliged for this assistance?).* These distinctions are observed less and less in current English. The usage cited above is characteristic of formal editing and is generally followed in edited prose. In natural informal speech, however, "whom" is quite rare. "Whom" still prevails as the object of a preposition when the preposition immediately precedes *(all patients with whom you have had contact),* but this juxtaposition tends to be avoided in both speech and writing, esp. in questions *(Who is this gift from?)* and sometimes by omission of the pronoun altogether *(all patients you have had contact with).*

REDUNDANCIES

It seems that so much writing is rife with redundancies these days. The most common one I see is "reason why." Say "It is the reason I told you that" or "It is why I told you that" instead of "It is the *reason why* I told you that." You don't need both words.

Avoid tautologizing as much as you can. Tautology is the needless repetition of an idea in different words, as in "widow woman." Good writing is taut (tidy, neat, trim), not tautologous.

Here's a list of redundancies that appear often, not only in everyday conversation and in writer's manuscripts, but in newspapers, magazines, and even on television newscasts.

absolutely certain	actual fact	added bonus
just exactly	radiate out	raise up
revert back	regular routine	resume again
reiterate again	right-hand side	left-hand side
alternative choice	may possibly be	meet together
minute detail	same identical	separate out
and also	completely full	sum total
deadly killer	drop down	fatal suicide
enter into	time when	protrude out
previous history	forward progress	baby kitten
annual birthday	follow behind	cash money

CONSISTENCY

Check for tense. If you are writing in present tense, be sure that you don't slip into past tense.

Once you decide on a style, stick with it. *Style* is defined as the rules of uniformity in punctuation, capitalization, spelling, word division and other details of expression. They often vary according to custom. Textbook publishers require a different style than publishers of romance novels, for example. Knowing the styles they use and abiding by them will make you appear more experienced in that field of writing.

Your voice and the voice of your characters should also be consistent. When you are writing nonfiction, don't move back and forth between formal and informal speech. If you are writing a novel and you give your character an accent, stay with it throughout the book. If he usually says "I ain't" don't have him sometimes saying "I'm not."

REPETITION

Once you have stated a character's title, described how she

looks or what he does, don't do it again unless you have a good reason. If you feel that it's important to remind the reader who this person is, say it differently, put a new twist on it.

In writing a how-to book such as this one, some repetitions are necessary. There are issues touched upon in earlier chapters that need elaboration in others. For example, in the chapters on book proposals and query letters, I will be explaining some of the things mentioned before. That is because they bear repeating in a different context.

FLOW, CONTINUITY AND TRANSITIONS

In writing, **flow** means to proceed continuously, smoothly or easily.

Continuity is defined as a continuous or connected whole.

A **transition** is a passage that links one scene or topic to another.

After you have done all the editing you can, read your entire manuscript through from start to finish at one sitting, if possible, keeping these guidelines in mind. Does it **flow** or are there words, phrases or ideas that create snags along the way?

Do you keep going back and forth in time and, if so, is it really necessary? Maintaining a logical **continuity** helps the flow and makes it easier for the reader to follow.

When you begin a new sentence or paragraph, is it jarring, does it seem to skip a beat or to make too big a jump in the storyline? Is it too abrupt a change of subject? Good **transitions** can cure that problem.

William Zinsser advises, "Learn to alert the reader as soon as possible to any change in mood from the previous sentence. . . . Many of us were taught that no sentence should begin with 'but.' If that's what you learned, unlearn it—there's no stronger word at the start." I agree with him. You might have noticed that I start a lot of sentences in this book with *but* or *and.*

Transitions are also important when ending one chapter and starting another. Here's an example from *Island* by Aldous Huxley; at the end of Chapter 14, a character named Susila is speaking:

> "The *moksha*-medicine can take you to heaven; but it can also take you to hell. Or else to both, together or alternately. Or else (if you're lucky, or if you've made yourself ready) beyond either of them. And then beyond the beyond, back to where you started from—back to here, back to New Rothamsted, back to business as usual. Only now, of course, business as usual is completely different."

That last sentence hooks the reader and signals that something is about to change. Chapter 15 begins like this:

> One, two, three, four . . . the clock in the kitchen struck twelve. How irrelevantly, seeing that time had ceased to exist!

Great writers know how to create page-turners. It would be hard to put *Island* down for the night after reading the last sentence of Chapter 14. Huxley was a gifted storyteller but he was also a craftsman. And craft is something we can all learn even if creativity isn't.

Being aware of the above principles and making the necessary adjustments along the way can help make your writing more readable, interesting, and professional looking.

QUOTATIONS AND PUNCTUATION MARKS

How to use quotations within quotations and punctuation with quotation marks can be confusing. But here are some generally accepted rules.

Double quotation marks are used in text to enclose quoted words, phrases, and sentences. Single quotation marks are used for quotations within quotations. And quotations within those single quotation marks should be double quotation marks again. Here's an example:

> "Alice," Mom explained, "your dad didn't say you could borrow the car, period. He said, 'Alice may use the car only if she comes to me and says, "I'm sorry I dented the fender and I promise to get it fixed"!' "

The ending punctuation is placed according to the person it belongs to. Mom is saying what Dad said he wanted to hear Alice say. As the exclamation point belongs to Dad's speech, it goes inside the single quotation mark. There should be no other punctuation marks at the end.

Commas and periods always come before a close quote.

> Where once we called people from that part of the world "Orientals," we now refer to them as "Asians."

A semicolon should be placed outside quotation marks or parentheses.

> William Faulkner once said, "Really, the writer doesn't want success"; that's not my reason for writing either. When the day comes that I must "pass through that wall of oblivion" I'll be content just to leave a scratch on it.

Colons, exclamation points, and question marks are usually placed inside quotation marks. For example:

> Tina Turner's hit was "What's Love Got to Do with It?"

And from *Strange Fits of Passion* by William Wordsworth:

> "What fond and wayward thoughts will slide
> Into a Lover's head!
> 'O mercy!' to myself I cried,
> 'If Lucy should be dead!'"

Only rarely is the **quotation mark** placed before the ending punctuation, but you may see this and it isn't necessarily wrong:

> Who was called "the voice"?

Above all, be concise and clear. Even if you are writing a scholarly work, it will be a lot more interesting if you don't try to use every five-syllable word you know. Do you want to show off your vocabulary or do you want to communicate an idea? Consider this sentence:

> Debilitating practices of procrastination, inappropriate decisions, and inconsistent productivity led to the administrative termination of Oldham.

What did that mean and did you even care? It might be better to say *Oldham got fired because he put things off, made bad decisions, and wasn't very productive.* Another thing wrong with the sentence is that it is in the passive voice. The active voice is so much more interesting.

When you edit your work, see how many words you can take out. Fewer words, fewer syllables, and shorter sentences make better writing.

There used to be a clear division between styles for writing and styles for speaking. That is no longer the case except in some forms of formal writing such as scientific papers and some academic works. But they could also gain by striving for simplicity and clarity over pedantry.

Styles have changed so much in the past decade or so

that many of the rules we once followed are no longer valid.

In checking what the *Chicago Manual of Style, 14th Edition* (published in 1993) had to say about split infinitives, I found this interesting footnote to Section 2.98 *Watching for errors and infelicities:*

> The thirteenth edition [1982] of this manual included split infinitives among the examples of 'errors and infelicities' but tempered the inclusion by adding, in parentheses, that they are 'debatable "errors." ' The item has been dropped from the fourteenth edition because the Press now regards the intelligent and discriminating use of the construction as a legitimate form of expression and nothing writers or editors need feel uneasy about. Indeed, it seems to us that in many cases clarity and naturalness of expression are best served by a judicious splitting of infinitives.

We can now split infinitives, end sentences in prepositions, and even dangle participles without being in error as long as we are clear.

WORKING WITH AN EDITOR

Having someone with experience go over your work can be very beneficial. It's hard to be objective about your own writing and hard to see your own errors. Even though I am an editor, I need editing. My work is always improved after an editor has been through it.

If you decide to hire an editor, make sure that you get someone who is qualified. Find out if the editor has worked on books before. You may want to talk to authors who have worked with an editor on their books or get references from agents or small publishers.

If you can't find someone with experience in editing books, an English teacher or a published writer might be good choices. Be aware, though, that not all English teachers are creative writers and not all writers can edit.

Ask what the editor charges and whether she is willing to edit a few pages so that you can see what kind of work she does. Don't expect anyone to do that free of charge. Make arrangements to pay her for three or four hours of work. Then she can get an idea of how long it will take to edit your entire book and can give you an estimate of the total charge. She should also be able to give you some excellent feedback at that point so that you may do some corrections yourself before you go on.

Getting an editor means you have to turn over your "baby" to someone who may not be as kind as you are to it. It's hard to keep our egos out of our writing. If you are arguing with the editor, any number of things may be going on. She may be making too many changes. You may be trying to hold onto every word. You may be having a personality conflict with the editor and she may not be the right one for you to work with.

An editor should be clear and honest about how he thinks your work should be changed. However, there is no excuse for insensitivity or harsh, negative criticism. A good editor will make suggestions, not pronouncements.

The editor should not rewrite your book or change your voice. He should have the ability to guide you and help you organize your work. He should make grammatical, punctuation, and spelling corrections, and show you how you can improve the flow of your work.

How you relate to the editor will have an effect on the outcome of your manuscript. If you go into the relationship with the attitude that you want your book to be the best it can be, if you can remain open to his suggestions and changes and keep your ego out of the process, you will very likely end up with a much better manuscript that you started out with.

Whether you are working with an editor you hire or one who works for your publisher, recognize the fact that the editor is there to make you look good. A professional editor wants to help your book become the best it can be. Having the opportunity to discuss with the editor the changes he has made, whether or not you agree with them, can make you see your work in a new light and move your writing forward in giant steps.

Chapter Five

THE A-PLUS PRESENTATION

*With regard to excellence, it is not enough to know,
but we must try to have and use it.*

—Aristotle

The A-Plus Presentation involves excellence in appearance and attitude. Whether it is a query letter, a book proposal, a synopsis, a treatment, or your entire manuscript, it should be of high quality and presented in a professional manner. After all, your work is a part of you. It is one indication of who you are. As you are preparing your work, consider these principles of presentation. Whenever you are speaking with an agent, publisher or anyone in the publishing field, you need to present yourself as a professional.

The principles apply to many areas of life, but these

guidelines are specifically for you and your written works.

APPEARANCE

Your appearance is your first impression, the first thing anyone sees. If you were looking for a job you would want to be neat, clean and appropriately dressed. Your written presentation needs to be all of these as well. Often the over-all appearance of your manuscript will determine whether your work will be taken seriously. The more professional looking your work is, the more likely it will be read. Here are some pointers:

> ➢ Always send fresh copies of your work. Do not send copies that have been returned to you from other presentations if they have been damaged or look shopworn. No one wants to think that she was not the first choice or important enough to warrant a good copy.

> ➢ Make generous margins. They should be at least one-inch on all sides. This is more inviting to the eye and easier to read. Narrow margins make it look like you tried to cram a lot of information into a small space. Framed with wider margins, the page itself is more appealing.

> ➢ Format your presentation appropriately. Use the style prevailing in the field for which you are presenting it. For instance, business letters and the synopsis of your book should be single-spaced. The rest of the book proposal and your manuscript should be double-spaced. A treatment (which is like a synopsis only longer) for film or

television should be double-spaced.

➤ The print should be sharp and dark enough to read easily. If you can, avoid a typewriter or a dot matrix printer. Inkjet or laser printers are best. Use a font or typeface that is easy to read. Times New Roman or some variation of it is good. And it should be in 12 point. Anything smaller is also hard to read.

➤ Edit and proofread your work several times. Check it for misspellings, grammatical errors, overly long sentences or paragraphs, misplaced punctuation and so forth.

➤ Don't send your work out the day you write it. Read it carefully again the next day or a week later to be sure that you are sending out your cleanest, clearest and most interesting presentation.

ATTITUDE

Choose carefully the person and company you send your query, book proposal, or manuscript to. Do your research to ascertain whether they are appropriate for what you have written. It will save the agent/publisher the time and trouble of dealing with an author who does not write what they represent/publish. It will also save you time and embarrassment. Then, when you do contact them, maintain a professional and courteous attitude.

The tone of your query letter and of any interview should be upbeat and positive. Be yourself but be the best self you can be. Here are some suggestions.

➤ Maintain a professional relationship with the

agent or publisher you are dealing with. Stick to the facts of your works, career and professional experience. Don't discuss personal problems. Don't gossip or bad-mouth his competitor (who may have already turned you down). People in the book publishing industry often know, talk to, and even like each other.

➤ Be friendly and open, not overly formal. Relax and let your personality come through.

➤ Be courteous. Even if the person you wish to impress isn't, even if she doesn't recognize the fact that you have written the first great novel of the 21st century, and even if he doesn't have time to discuss your manuscript in depth. If the agent or publisher does not want your book, that's no reason to be rude. You may wish to present something else to this person someday. It would be wise to leave a good impression.

➤ Don't apologize and don't be defensive. If there is something in your work or your presentation of it that requires an elaborate explanation or an apology, then it isn't ready to be sent out. Keep all negative comments out of your communications. Maintain a positive attitude and it will show through in all that you do.

➤ Project confidence. It's not a good idea to praise your own work highly—how can you be objective when you are so close to it—but you can exhibit self-assurance and present yourself and your work in the best possible light.

➤ If you get a face-to-face meeting with a publisher, dress for business. That means no cut-off jeans or low-cut blouses. Even though you are a writer and everyone knows that writers are eccentric, for this first meeting at least, be presentable, be on time, and be prepared.

➤ Don't be emotional. Don't threaten to slash your wrists or their tires if they turn down your manuscript. Neither anger nor self-pity will get you a publishing contract.

Maybe you already know how to present yourself and you didn't need those tips. But not all writers are as stable as you. And believe it or not, publishers have told me that people actually have threatened to kill themselves or worse, they've threatened to kill the publisher. There are some pretty nutty people out there.

Chapter Six

COPYRIGHT INFORMATION

Take away from English authors their copyrights, and you would very soon take away from England her authors.

—Anthony Trollope, 1815-1882

Copyright law did not exist until the invention of the printing press in Europe in the 15th century. Before that it was expensive and very time-consuming to produce a book and few people knew how to read anyway.

When books became cheaper and more widely available, the royal government of England granted a group of book publishers called the London Stationers' Company a monopoly on the printing of books. However, the purpose of this early form of copyright wasn't to protect author's and publisher's rights. It was to raise revenue and give the government control over the contents of the publications. And it was effective. The publishers, not wishing to risk the loss of their monopoly, only published materials that were approved by the royal authorities.

THE HISTORY OF COPYRIGHT LAWS

The first real copyright law, in the modern sense, was passed in England in 1710. Called the Statute of Anne (named for Queen Anne), it granted authors the exclusive right to have their books printed for a limited duration. After 28 years, the works could pass into public domain. Similar laws were enacted in the 18th century in Denmark and France.

In 1790, the United States Congress adopted the nation's first copyright law. Congress made a major revision to it in the Copyright Act of 1909, reacting to new inventions such as photography and motion pictures. It was replaced by the Copyright Act of 1976 and, although the act has been amended often since then, this statute remains the legal basis for copyright protection in the United States.

SHOULD YOU REGISTER YOUR COPYRIGHT?

Yes. It offers you protections you can't get any other way. You may have heard that to prove authorship you can put your manuscript into a large manila envelope and send it to yourself. And when it arrives, don't open it; just file it away. That method of "protection" may cost less than a copyright registration but I advise against it and so do attorneys. Why take a risk when it costs only $30 to register your copyright? If your manuscript has taken a year or two (or more) out of your life to write, doesn't it deserve the maximum legal protection you can give it?

THE ADVANTAGES OF COPYRIGHT REGISTRATION

There are some distinct advantages to registering your copyright with the Copyright Office.

➤ It establishes a public record of your copyright claim.

➤ You may not file an infringement suit in court unless your works have been registered.

➤ Registration establishes *prima facie* evidence in court of the validity of the copyright.

➤ A timely registration will allow you (the copyright owner) to seek damages and attorney's fees. Otherwise, only actual damages and profits are available to the author.

➤ The registration may be filed with the U.S. Customs Service to provide protection from the importation of infringing copies.

Mailing yourself a copy of your manuscript will not give you any of those protections. The above information and a great deal more is in **Circular 1, Copyright Basics,** published by the U.S. Copyright Office.

WHAT A COPYRIGHT IS

The Copyright Office describes a copyright as a form of protection provided by the law (title 17, U.S. Code) to authors of "original works of authorship" including literary, dramatic, musical, artistic, and certain other intellectual works. It is available both for published and unpublished works. Section 106 of the 1976 Copyright Act generally gives the owner of the copyright the exclusive right to do and to authorize others to do the following:

> ➤ Reproduce the copyrighted work in copies or phonorecords

> ➤ Prepare derivative works based upon the copyrighted work

> ➤ Distribute copies of it to the public by sale or other transfer of ownership, or by rental, lease, or lending

> ➤ Perform and/or display the copyrighted work publicly

It is illegal for anyone to violate any of the rights provided by the Copyright Office to the owner of copyright. These rights, however, are not unlimited in scope. One major limitation is the doctrine of "fair use." There are certain circumstances in which parts of a work may be quoted.

The Copyright Office provides information on fair use in **Circular 21** and **FL102**. If your question is not clearly answered in either of those publications, check with an attorney familiar with fair use or request permission from the author and/or publisher of the works you wish to use.

Another limitation takes the form of "compulsory license" and has to do with limited uses upon payment of royalties and compliance with statutory conditions. For more information on these issues, consult the copyright law.

You can get this and other information from the Copyright Office by calling **(202) 707-3000** between 8:30 a.m. and 5:00 p.m. Eastern time, Monday through Friday. Their Web site is **www.loc.gov/copyright**.

THE COPYRIGHT FORMS

The Copyright Office provides application forms for various types of registrations. Form PA is used for works of the performing arts. Form SE is for serials such as newspapers, magazines, newsletters, etc. Form SR is for sound recordings. Form VA is for visual arts.

What we are concerned with here is **Form TX** and **Short Form TX**. These are the forms for registering nondramatic literary works including fiction, nonfiction, poetry, contributions to collective works, compilations, directories, catalogs, dissertations, theses, reports, speeches, bound or looseleaf volumes, pamphlets, brochures, and single pages containing text.

You may obtain copies of these forms by writing the Copyright Office or by downloading them from their Web site. Any copies you make, however, must look like the original. They must be clear and printed back to back and head to head using both sides of a single sheet of white paper that is 8½ x 11 inches in size. Short forms are one sided.

Use **Short Form TX** if:

➢ you are the **only** author and copyright owner of the work

➢ the work is completely new

➢ the work was **not** made for hire

➢ you are **not** registering under a pseudonym or pen name

Send the following three items, all in one package:

1. One nonreturnable copy of your work

2. A completed application (Form TX)

3. A check or money order for $30 nonrefundable filing fee payable to Register of Copyrights

Send to: Library of Congress
Copyright Office
101 Independence Avenue, S.E.
Washington, DC 20559-6000

REGISTRATION FEE

Please note that the registration fee has gone up. On July 1, 1999 the filing fee was raised from $20 to $30. This fee will be in effect through June 30, 2002.

You are not required to have your submission (manuscript) printed and you may use any paper size. To facilitate handling and long-term storage, it would be a good idea to staple, clip or bind it in some way. This brings up another interesting provision of the copyright law called "mandatory deposit."

MANDATORY DEPOSIT

You are required to send two copies of the best edition of your copyrightable work within three months of publication.

"Best edition" is defined as the copy of the highest quality. For example, if you have loose manuscript pages of your book as well as a bound edition, your "best edition" is the one that is bound.

"Publication" is defined in the copyright law as "the distribution of copies or phonorecords of a work to the public by sale or other transfer of ownership, or by rental, lease, or lending."

Deposits should be sent to:

Library of Congress
Register of Copyrights
Attn: 407 Deposits
101 Independence Avenue, S.E.
Washington, DC 20559-6000

While deposits for the collections of the Library of Congress are mandatory, registration of a copyright claim is not. To satisfy the requirements of both the mandatory deposit and the copyright registration, you'll need to send all of the following in the same package:

1. **Two** complete copies of the **best edition** of your work

2. A completed application (Form TX)

3. A $30 nonrefundable filing fee payable to the Register of Copyrights.

Although you will not be sent an acknowledgment that your application has been received, you may get a letter or phone call if they need additional information. Your certificate of registration will be sent within about eight months.

You may send your application package by registered or certified mail requesting a return receipt if you want to have proof that it arrived. If your registration is rejected you will get a letter explaining why.

REGISTERING UNDER A PSEUDONYM OR PEN NAME

You may use a pseudonym or pen name when registering your copyright, but the pseudonym itself is not protected by copyright. If you are writing under a pseudonym but want to be identified by your legal name in the copyright records, give your legal name followed by your pseudonym in space 2, "Name and Address of Author and Owner of the Copyright."

Example: "Samuel Langhorne Clemens whose pseudonym is Mark Twain."

Also check "yes" in the box next to "Pseudonymous?" at space 2. If you do not wish your identity revealed in the records, give your pseudonym and identify it as such.

Example: "Mark Twain, pseudonym."

You may also leave the space blank but you still must identify the citizenship or domicile of the author. You may use a pseudonym in space 4 but **do not** leave this space blank. However, be warned that if you hold your copyright under a fictitious name, you may have problems proving ownership in any business dealings. It's best to consult an attorney in this case. And you **must** sign Form TX in space 8. **Do not** use Short Form TX.

WHAT CANNOT BE COPYRIGHTED?

➤ Works that have not been fixed in a tangible form of expression, such as improvised speeches, dances, or music that has not been written or recorded

➤ Ideas, procedures, methods, systems, processes, concepts, principles, discoveries or devices, as distinguished from a description, explanation, or illustration

➤ Titles, names, short phrases and slogans; familiar symbols or designs; variations of lettering or coloring; lists of ingredients or contents

> ➤ Works consisting entirely of information that is common property and containing no original authorship, such as calendars, height and weight charts, tape measures and rulers, and lists or tables taken from public documents or other common sources

IS A NOTICE OF COPYRIGHT REQUIRED?

Under U.S. law a copyright notice is no longer required but it is still a good idea to indicate that your work is copyrighted. Use of the notice identifies the copyright owner and the first year of publication. If a proper notice of copyright appears on the published work, no one can claim they didn't know the work was protected.

The use of the copyright notice is your responsibility. You don't need permission from the Copyright Office to use it. And you do not have to register it first. The notice should contain all of the following:

> ➤ the symbol © or the word "Copyright" or the abbreviation "Copr." and

> ➤ the year of first publication of the work, and

> ➤ the name of the owner of the copyright

Example: © 2000 John Doe

HOW TO REACH THE COPYRIGHT OFFICE

For general information, you may call the Copyright Public Information Office at (202) 707-3000.

For specific application forms and circulars call Forms and Publications Hotline at (202) 707-9100.

Information by fax (but not application forms) is available by Fax-on-Demand at (202) 707-2600.

For information by regular mail, write to:

Library of Congress
Copyright Office
Publications Section, LM-455
101 Independence Avenue, S.E.
Washington, DC 20559-6000

Chapter Seven

LITERARY AGENTS

An agent may play a great many roles in the life and work of an author.... But an agent is, above all, a salesperson.
—Jonathan Kirsch, *Kirsch's Guide to the Book Contract*

As in all professions, there are good agents and there a bad agents. A bad agent is worse than none at all. Before you begin looking for a literary agent, you should know a few facts so that you can determine whether having representation will be in your best interests. The type of book you are writing and how it will be distributed may influence your decision. You may find that an agent is unnecessary and may only get in your way.

If you decide that you must have an agent, this chapter will provide you with information on finding a qualified agent who is best suited for you and your work.

DO YOU NEED AN AGENT?

The answer to that question depends on several factors. If you already have access to a publisher or publishers who are likely to want to publish your book you may not need an agent. If you know the book publishing business well you may prefer to hire a lawyer to help you negotiate your contract or do so yourself. Although you would have to pay a lawyer a fee, you wouldn't have to share your royalties with her as you would with an agent. However, if you want to reach a major publisher such as Simon & Schuster or Random House you must have an agent represent you. They rarely deal directly with an author before the contract is signed.

Smaller houses will accept queries and book proposals from individual authors; in fact, some prefer to deal with an author who does not have an agent.

The big advances you may have heard about in the past are a thing of the past. The new reality is that even major publishers do not offer large advances anymore unless you are a proven author who regularly sells books in the hundreds of thousands.

Since the smaller publishers often do not give authors any advance, an agent is reluctant to represent an author who will appeal only to small publishers. Fifteen percent of nothing is still nothing. The agent won't realize any financial remuneration until your royalties start to roll in and that could take years.

There are clear advantages and disadvantages to having a literary agent.

THE ADVANTAGES

Agents are more likely to get you an offer from a publisher than you are yourself. After all, that is their specialty. They will probably get you a larger advance and bigger royalties than you could negotiate for yourself, as well as a more advantageous contract all around. Qualified agents know what to watch for in a publishing contract and how to protect your rights. Jonathan Kirsch, an attorney specializing in intellectual property matters and publishing law, and author of *Kirsch's Guide to the Book Contract,* advises:

> An experienced agent will be far more adept, insightful and effective in dealing with the legal technicalities of a book contract than an attorney who lacks long and specific experience in the book publishing industry.

Experienced agents know which publishers buy the kind of book you are writing. They may already have a relationship with particular publishers through placing other books with them. Good agents may also nurture new authors and help guide their career.

THE DISADVANTAGES

You will probably be required to give the agent 15% of your advance and royalties. The check is mailed to your agent who takes his percentage out and then sends you the remaining amount.

Some publishers simply will not deal with an agent at all.

Once you have signed with an agent, you may not be able a deal with a publisher on your own. If you have signed an agreement with the agent for representation for a period of two years, for example, and the agent does nothing for you, it may be complicated for you to get out of that relationship.

If you choose not to have a literary agent represent you, you should have an attorney who specializes in intellectual property and/or entertainment law look over any publishing contract that is offered you. You may want to do that even if you do have an agent because the contract may be complex and beyond the area of expertise of an agent. However, according to Kirsch, "few book contracts are reviewed by *any* lawyer unless the dollar amounts are especially large or the legal issues are unusually problematic." One of the benefits of membership in the National Writers Union is contract advice for writers dealing with an agent or publisher. They also provide members with the NWU Preferred Literary Agent Agreement.

Some literary agents specialize in representing authors of books and may not have any connections with the television or film industry. If they don't have experience analyzing and negotiating TV and film deals, you may need a separate agent for that. If you have written a script or a treatment (synopsis) for a proposed film or television production it would be better for you to find an agent who deals mainly with that industry and is signatory to the Writers Guild of America (WGA).

HOW DO AGENTS GET NEW CLIENTS?

There are several ways agents get clients. These are the major ones, in order of frequency and likelihood.

➤ Through referrals. These may come from existing clients, editors, other agents, published authors or experts in a particular field.

➤ Through their speaking engagements at writers conferences and seminars.

➤ Through written queries from authors.

If you have met an agent through a seminar, a business

associate or some other way in which you have made personal contact, it is not inappropriate to call him/her and ask if you may send a query letter. If the agent is not too busy, you may even have the opportunity to pitch your idea over the phone.

HOW DO YOU FIND AN AGENT?

To look for an agent, check *Literary Market Place* published by R.R. Bowker, *Guide to Literary Agents* published by Writer's Digest Books or *The Insider's Guide to Book Editors, Publishers & Literary Agents* by Jeff Herman, published by Prima Communications. *Writer's Market* now lists agents but the listing is not extensive. The listings in the above guides are not to be considered recommendations because some of them are "business card" agents and may not be experienced or reputable.

Get the latest issue of the guides because agents move, go out of business, or are otherwise not available from year to year. Some of the above have Web sites and you may be able to do much of your research over the Internet.

In these guides you will find which agents represent the type of book you have written. Like publishers, many agents specialize in a particular genre such as how-to, spirituality, health, mysteries, etc. Because nonfiction books are easier to sell than novels, especially by first-time authors, most agents represent nonfiction writers. If you are a novelist, you may have a tougher time finding a literary agent. The closer you can match the agent to the type of book you are writing, the better chance you will have that she will be interested in representing you and your book.

Before you contact any agents, notice whether they want to be queried first or will accept a synopsis or a book proposal along with your query or cover letter. Very few will want to look at a complete manuscript on first contact.

HOW DO YOU CHOOSE THE *RIGHT* AGENT?

Whenever possible, get recommendations from authors, publishers, editors or others who have dealt with the agent.

An agent may suggest that your manuscript would have a better chance of being accepted by a publisher if you have it edited. That may be a valid comment as most manuscripts do need professional editing. But beware if the agent refers you to a specific company. They may know of a good editor but some agents receive referral fees from editing companies and may be more interested in collecting their fee than in helping you. In such cases, the agent may not agree to represent you even after your book has been edited. You could end up spending a lot of money on an editor who is not right for your book.

Some agents charge a reading fee of up to $450. As that may be a major source of income for them rather than a percentage of your advance and royalties, they may not be operating in your best interests.

For information on qualified agents, check with the Association of Authors' Representatives and the National Writers Union who require literary agents to be qualified and to abide by a high standard of ethics to be listed with them. The Writers Guild of America requires the agent to be a signatory to their organization.

WHAT TO WATCH OUT FOR

Although the AAR does not accept agents who charge reading fees, there are a few fee-charging agents who are legitimate and render a valuable service to writers. But picking a good one out of the crowd is hard to do. If an agent merely reads your manuscript and then passes on it you will have learned nothing. Some agents will send a report and then ask for an additional fee for a more detailed analysis. That practice is highly suspect. If you think you have found a responsible, ethical fee-charging agent and decide to send your material to her, be sure that you will get something in return. Ask the following questions:

➢ What services do you provide for the reading fee?

➢ Will my material be evaluated by someone with professional experience?

➢ Will I receive a detailed report with some editorial suggestions and the marketability for this type of book?

➢ How long before I receive a report?

➢ What is the fee for a complete analysis?

➢ If you decide to accept me as a client will the fee be refunded?

Don't be afraid to ask for information from the agent about his charges, method of working, clients' published books and experience. Remember, the agent is paid by you, not the other way around. You have a right to know everything about him that will help you in your selection.

It is very important to choose the right agent; one who not only is ethical and experienced but is someone you feel rapport with. The National Writers Union gets many complaints from writers who have been defrauded and mistreated by agents. Many so-called agents are nothing but scam artists. Literary agents are not regulated by any governmental agency and don't have to have any experience, knowledge or training to call themselves agents. Script agents who are signatory to the Writers Guild of America, however, must abide by a standard code of behavior.

Although you may want to get a list of agents from the Association of Authors' Representatives, there are other organizations that can give you valuable information on specific agents.

The National Writers Union maintains an Agents Database. However, it is available only to NWU members. Many working writers join the NWU because of the benefits and protections they offer that are not available to writers anywhere else.

The Agent Research & Evaluation Company tracks agents in court records and the press. They've been around since 1980 and have a good reputation. They sell reports from their database and you can get a summary on an agent from them. AR&E is at 334 E. 30th Street, New York, NY 10016.

The Fisher Report publishes a list of disreputable agents. Write to Prof. Jim Fisher at Edinboro University, Dept. of Political Science and Criminal Justice, Hendricks Hall, Edinboro, PA 16444 for information on how to get a copy of the Fisher Report.

The American Society of Journalists and Authors reports problems with agents from time to time in their Contract Watch. The address for the ASJA is 1501 Broadway, Suite 302, New York, NY 10036.

Once you have decided on which agents to query—and you may want to choose several—you can begin to compose your letter, customizing it to fit each particular agent. (See chapter on Query Letters.)

Chapter Eight

THE BOOK PROPOSAL

Oh, that my words were now written! oh that
they were printed in a book.

—Job 19:23

*H*ave you ever said, "But I'm an author—an art-
ist—my job is to write. Why do I need to prepare
a book proposal?" I think most writers feel that
way; I certainly do. In a perfect world, we could be authors
who just write and get discovered by publishers who sell
thousands of our books and make us rich and famous. Un-
fortunately, we live in an imperfect world. We have to work
at making ourselves known to those who are in the business
of publishing the kinds of books we write. We need to con-
vince publishers that they will benefit by publishing our
book. But even that isn't enough. We will then have to con-

vince book buyers that they will enjoy reading it. That means we need to do a book proposal.

A BOOK PROPOSAL IS LIKE A BUSINESS PLAN

It is a sales tool. Suppose you had invented a robotic maid and wanted it to be carried by a department store chain that would sell it to their customers. But they already carry a robotic maid in their housewares section; several brands, in fact. What's different and better about yours? Well, like the others, yours cleans the house but, unlike the others, it also does windows. Not only that, yours makes lunch and laughs at your jokes. But that department store isn't going to know all that unless you tell them. You could give them a call but in the end they will want to see some promotional material and possibly a demonstration. They'll have to be convinced that there are people out there who will be interested in owning your particular robotic maid. It's your job to sell them on this wondrous machine.

It's not that much different when your product is a book. Writing a query letter isn't enough. It may get a publisher interested but he will still want a demonstration. He will want to know more about your book and whether there is a market for it. He'll ask to see a book proposal and sample chapters or, sometimes, the entire manuscript.

For nonfiction, you can think of an idea, gather the facts, organize the material, write a couple of chapters, prepare a book proposal and find out if a publisher will be interested before you even write the book.

An excellent resource is *Write the Perfect Book Proposal* by Jeff Herman and Deborah M. Adams. One of the features I particularly like about this book is, as the subtitle says, it contains *10 Proposals that Sold and Why*. In their Introduction, the authors state:

Thousands of writers each year fail to find a publisher because they write mediocre proposals, even though many of them would have gone on to write successful books. The proposal process must be taken seriously; it's the price of admission to being a published author.

While the query letter for a novel and a nonfiction book are essentially the same, the book proposal format presented here is designed primarily for the nonfiction book.

A book proposal for fiction does not contain as many parts. The proposal for a novel might have only the title page, a synopsis and an author bio. If the author has written other books they should be listed along with information on how well they sold. Although there are exceptions, most agents and publishers want to see the entire manuscript of a novel rather than sample chapters. A novel is a much tougher sell than a nonfiction book.

A query letter should not be sent out until your book proposal has been completed. If you get a request from an agent or publisher to see your proposal, it should be ready so that you can send it right away. Their interest may evaporate if you let a few weeks or months go by.

The advantages of writing a book proposal before you write the book are many. As you go through all the steps of the proposal you will learn:

> **how to focus on your subject.** If you have a descriptive title and can sum up your book in one short sentence, you probably have a clear idea of what your book is about.

> **how to describe your book to others.** By writing a synopsis, you will be able to get to the essence of the information contained in your book and explain it clearly.

> ➤ **how to organize your material.** Preparing a chapter-by-chapter outline of your book will help keep you on track as your write.

> ➤ **whether you have a salable idea.** As you research the market potential, you will find out if your book is likely to find a wide audience.

> ➤ **how to sell yourself.** You will discover your qualifications for writing your book when you tell about your background and promotional skills. You can then build upon your strengths and do additional research in areas where you lack training or experience.

> ➤ **what your competition is** and if there are other books on the same subject. If you find books that are similar to yours, you may want to change yours in some way or re-think whether you want to write it.

Whether you have already written a nonfiction book or are contemplating writing one you will need to know what it takes to sell it. A book proposal can be prepared no matter what stage of writing you are currently in. There are several factors that make for a best-selling nonfiction book. If you address all of these issues carefully and your book meets most of the following criteria, your chances of getting published will be greatly improved.

WHAT MAKES A NONFICTION BOOK SUCCESSFUL?

> ➤ The subject is timely and/or timeless, it is unique or presented in a unique way, it is interesting and appeals to a wide audience.

➢ The title is descriptive, invites inquiry, shocks or soothes or in some way attracts attention.

➢ It is well-written and carefully edited with attention paid to spelling, grammar and sentence structure.

➢ It avoids scientific or technical terminology unfamiliar to the layperson. It is easy to read.

➢ The author is a professional in the field about which he is writing, is considered an authority on the subject, or has done extensive research on it.

➢ The material is well-organized.

➢ The presentation is attractive, appealing and professional looking.

➢ It has been diligently promoted and marketed.

Prepare your Book Proposal with all of the above factors in mind. The last item may not seem to be of concern to you as the author. But it is, because you will have to help promote and, in some cases, market your book no matter who the publisher is.

The format may differ somewhat depending on the publisher or agent to whom you will be presenting your proposal. For instance, some publishers require one sample chapter, some three or even more.

Some agents may ask that you put your name on every page and others may ask you not to. It's a good idea to modify your book proposal according to the wishes of the person or company with whom you are dealing. You can find this information in a number of ways:

> ➤ by finding the publisher's listing in the latest issue of Writer's Market,

> ➤ by writing to the publisher and asking for guidelines,

> ➤ by checking out the publisher's Web site, and

> ➤ by calling the publisher and asking.

The entire book proposal should be double-spaced with the exception of the Synopsis. On each page, place the section number and subject in the upper right corner. Below that put the title of your book and under that the page number in that section.

THE BOOK PROPOSAL CONTENTS PAGE

It is helpful to have a table of contents that shows at a glance what you have included in your proposal. At the top of the page, type "Book Proposal for [the title of your book]" Below that list the sections of the book proposal you have included, a list of illustrations, if any, and note which illustrations you are enclosing. After that, state which chapters you are sending. On the following page is an example.

BOOK PROPOSAL FOR

_____

(title of book)

by _____

(name of author)

I.   Title Page

II.   Synopsis

III.   About the Author

IV.   Market Potential

V.   Competitive Works

VI.   Chapter Outline

VII.   List of Illustrations

Sample Illustrations
(note what illustrations are included)

Chapters _____
(note the chapter numbers included)

Author's name
Address, City, State and Zip
Telephone & fax number
E-mail address

I. TITLE PAGE

(Title and brief description of book)

Your title should be provocative and succinct. Short titles are usually preferred by publishers and they are easier for potential readers to remember. Notice how many books on bestseller lists have three-word titles. Although there are some exceptions, such as *Men are from Mars, Women are from Venus* and *How to Get What You Want and Want What You Have,* only rarely do books on those lists have more than six words in the title. You can add a subtitle if you think that your short title doesn't tell enough about the book.

Do your best to get a hook into the title; something that will grab attention. Engage the emotions as much as possible such as in these recent titles: *Yesterday I Cried, All Too Human, Reaching to Heaven, Soul of the Fire, Bittersweet, We'll Meet Again, The Courage to be Rich, Abide with Me.*

The title should convey in some way what your book is about, especially if it is nonfiction. Some examples of titles that do this are: *Emotional Intelligence, Dr. Atkin's New Diet Revolution, Slaves in the Family,* and *The Greatest Generation.*

Study the subject guide to *Books in Print* and note whether the subject you are writing on has been updated within the past few years. Also check *Forthcoming Books* which details the books that publishers currently have in the works. Both are published by R.R. Bowker Co. Many book stores and public libraries have these lists on their computer.

Choose a title that has not been used before. Even though you can use an existing title because titles cannot be copyrighted, you wouldn't want your book confused with someone else's. If you want yours to stand out, it's best to select a title that is unique. If there are several books on the subject you have chosen, be sure that yours is different in important ways.

On the Title Page, put your title and your name as the author. Below that write a brief description of your book. This is your primary sales pitch. Make it short and intriguing.

List the number of words or pages you have written or expect to write. An average double-spaced manuscript page has around 300 to 350 words. The number of words on a book page varies widely depending on the size of the font and the page and the width of the margins. Most nonfiction books are between 170 and 300 pages. If your book will have fewer or more pages than these, be sure that there is a good reason for it. If there are fewer pages, don't pad. Every word should have a reason to be there. If there are more than 300 pages, be sure that you have not repeated yourself and that it requires that many pages to make your points.

Number the pages of the book proposal according to the section they are in, starting with page one in each new section.

On the following page is the format for the Title Page.

I. TITLE PAGE
Title of Book

_____

(Title)

_____

(Subtitle)

By _____

(Author)

_____

_____

_____

(Brief description of book; one sentence, if possible)

Number of Pages: _____

II. Synopsis

This is an overview or brief summary of the book. It should be about 1½ to 2 pages long and single-spaced. Place the book proposal section number and name on the top right corner of the page. Below that, the title of you book, and under than the page number. Example:

> II. SYNOPSIS
> *This is My Life*
> Page 1

Having a focused idea and being able to explain it in a few short paragraphs is essential. Tell the purpose of your book and what it will do for the reader.

The lead paragraph must grab the interest of the acquisitions editor. Open with a powerful statement, startling statistics, or facts that will create an emotional reaction.

Read book reviews, especially those on a similar subject as yours, and study book jackets as guides in developing the tone of the synopsis. As some agents and acquisition editors may not read beyond this point, it is important that you make the synopsis not only informative but interesting.

The synopsis should have a beginning, middle and end, just as your book does. Tell how your book opens, what it is about, and how it ends. You may want to give some of the highlights, specific events, dialogue or unknown facts.

At the bottom of the page, estimate the time needed to complete the book once the contract is signed.

Try to touch on most of the following in your synopsis:

➢ What kind of book is it? Tell whether it is a how-to, mystery, children's book, poetry, cookbook, history, biography, etc.

➤ If it is a novel, what is the story? Who are the main characters?

➤ What is interesting and different about it? Is there an unusual twist? A unique point of view?

➤ How is it written? For example, if it is a novel, is it written in first person? If a nonfiction book, is it written for the layperson?

III. ABOUT THE AUTHOR

This is also called Author's Background and Promotional Skills or Biographical Information. It is a narrative statement of your qualifications, experience and reasons for writing the book. Do *not* send a resume or curriculum vitae. This should be one to two pages long.

Tell about yourself, list other books you have written, and explain your promotional skills such as public speaking, television or radio appearances, or seminars you have conducted on the subject. Suggest the names of prominent figures or authorities who may endorse your book. If you already have contacted them and they have agreed, be sure to mention it.

To see if you have covered everything, use the following checklist.

☐ Education

☐ Experience in the field you are writing about

☐ Other books, articles, scripts, or papers you have written

☐ Public speaking experience. Seminar presenter?
Teacher? Politician? Actor?

☐ Personal information, especially when applicable to
what you are writing

☐ Marketing or promotional experience

☐ Reason for writing this book

☐ Endorsements

All of the above may not apply to you and your book. If
you are writing a novel, a university degree may be unim-
portant. If you are writing a nonfiction book regarding a
specific field of interest it will be important to show that
you have training and/or experience in that field. Some
authors also send a picture of themselves but that is not
necessary.

IV. MARKET POTENTIAL

Research the demographics and statistics of potential readers. For example: "The number of women living with children whose father was absent was over 10 million as of
spring of 1996." This number will be significant if your
book is about how a single mother can help her child feel
secure, excel in school and make positive choices. These
single mothers are all potential readers.

If your book were about motorcycles, you would want to
have statistics on how many people own motorcycles. You
would also want to tell how many motorcycle clubs and
dealers there are because they are also potential readers
and your book may sell through their club or store.

Here's an example from a book proposal that attracted a

publisher who subsequently published the book. The book, *Code to Victory: The Fact and Fiction of "Y" Intelligence,* by Arnold C. Franco and Paula Aselin Spellman, was a memoir of an Air Force veteran of World War II. The research turned up a large number of organizations whose members are potential buyers of this book:

The American Legion; 3.1 million members

The American Legion Auxiliary; one million members

The Air Force Association; 180,000 members

American Veterans of WWII, Korea & Vietnam (AMVETS); 200,000 members

Veterans of Foreign Wars; 2,850,000 members

The 9th Air Force Association; 2,500 members

In addition to the usual bookstore, Internet and mail order outlets, this book probably would sell well in PXs, officers clubs, military base gift shops and at meetings, conventions and events presented each year by many military organizations. It would very likely get reviewed in military publications and be carried in military and historical libraries.

For my own first book, *A Woman's Way: the Stop Smoking Book for Women,* I did a lot of my research in hospital libraries and, among other important facts, found out how many American women are smoking, what percentage of them want to quit, the health statistics for female vs. male smokers and the health effects on the fetuses, infants and children of women smokers.

Among the outlets for this book was women's clinics,

gynecologist's offices, and hospitals were interested in stocking *A Woman's Way* for doctors, nurses, and therapists to give to their patients.

Debbie Puente, author of *Elegantly Easy Crème Brulee and Other Custard Desserts,* discovered after her book was published that she could sell quite a few books doing book signings in gourmet markets, cookware shops and other specialty stores. That kind of promotion virtually guarantees that those stores will carry the book.

Jean Wade, who wrote *How Sweet It Is . . . Without the Sugar,* a dessert cookbook for diabetics and people on low-sugar diets, was delighted to learn that her publisher sent her book for review to various magazines and periodicals dealing with health. Book reviews in major publications are even better than ads. She does book signings in grocery stores that subsequently stock her books at their checkout stands.

After an excellent review in CHOICE, Current Reviews for Academic Libraries, Stephen E. Blewett's book, *What's in the Air: Natural and Man-Made Air Pollution,* began selling steadily to public libraries and schools.

Knowing of these possible outlets for your book at the time you are preparing your book proposal gives you a distinct advantage. Don't assume that the publisher will know how and where to market your book. You may have ideas the publisher hasn't even thought of.

V. COMPETITIVE WORKS

Research other books on the same subject; this is your competition. Borrow or buy books which may be similar to yours and read them. Choose four or five and list each by title, author, publisher, the year published, the number of pages and the price. Write a brief synopsis of each one and explain how yours is different. Here's an example:

> **Codebreakers: The Inside Story of Bletchley Park,** by
> F. H. Hinsley (Editor) & Alan Stripp (Editor); Oxford
> University Press; October 1994; paperback, illustrated;
> 321 pages. $14.95
> Bletchley Park, the top secret workplace of the
> cryptanalysts who cracked Germany's Enigma Code, is
> considered by some World War II historians to be the
> most successful intelligence operation in world history.
> This book is closest to Arnold Franco's as it deals with
> breaking the code of the Germans during World War II.
> It gives 27 first-hand accounts written by the British
> and American members of the codebreakers' team.
> The above book differs in significant ways from
> **Code to Victory** which is a personal memoir of author
> Franco who served as a cryptanalyst in a mobile unit
> which was to function with the advancing armies. His
> book also recalls the stories of others in his unit but,
> rather than being a compilation of stories, it is Franco's
> first-person account that includes the experiences of
> others in his unit.

Be sure the books you list are recent. Very old books
will not be considered comparable.

VI. CHAPTER OUTLINE

Prepare a Table of Contents with chapter titles but without
page numbers. Under each chapter title write a paragraph
or two explaining what it is about. This indicates that you
have a clear grasp of your subject and have planned exactly
how and in what order you will present your information.
Here's an example from my book proposal:

> **Chapter 1: A Cigarette is NOT a Friend**
> Women often think of a cigarette as a friend; something

that is always there when they are nervous, emotionally upset, lonely or even celebrating. Smoking is a different addiction in women than it is in men. It is more damaging to their health and it's harder for them to quit.

Chapter 2: Pregnancy, PMS and Menopause
This chapter explains the danger to the fetus of a pregnant woman. It also tells how smoking can intensify premenstrual tension, and the increased tension like a vicious cycle, makes it harder for women to quit. There is evidence that smoking can also bring on an early menopause.

VII. LIST OF ILLUSTRATIONS
If you have photographs, drawings, graphs, charts, maps or other illustrations that will become a part of this work, list and describe each one. Also include samples.

SAMPLE CHAPTERS
You will be sending between one and three completed chapters, depending on what the publisher asks for. Always send the first chapter because publishers usually want to know how you get into your subject. The first ten pages of your book are crucial. Actually, the first page is crucial, even the first few lines. You must grab the reader's interest right away. Here are some lines from the first pages of best-selling novels:

> My father has asked me to be the fourth corner at the Joy Luck Club. I am to replace my mother, whose seat at the mah jong table has been empty since she died two months ago. My father thinks she was killed by her own thoughts.
> *The Joy Luck Club*, by Amy Tan

His two girls are curled together like animals whose

habit is to sleep underground, in the smallest space possible.

Animal Dreams, by Barbara Kingsolver

The large ballroom was crowded with familiar ghosts come to help celebrate her birthday. Kate Blackwell watched them mingle with the flesh-and-blood people, and in her mind, the scene was a dreamlike fantasy as the visitors from another time and place glided around the dance floor with the unsuspecting guests in black tie and long, shimmering evening gowns.

Master of the Game, by Sidney Sheldon

And these are from best-selling nonfiction books (memoirs):

My father and mother should have stayed in New York where they met and married and where I was born. . . . When I look back on my childhood I wonder how I survived at all.

Angela's Ashes, by Frank McCourt

As a boy, I never knew where my mother was from— where she was born, who her parents were. When I asked she'd say, "God made me." When I asked if she was white, she'd say, "I'm light-skinned," and change the subject. She raised twelve black children and sent us all to college..."

The Color of Water;
A Black Man's Tribute to His White Mother,
by James McBride

The most famous first line of all time is "It was the best of times, it was the worst of times" from the classic *A Tale of Two Cities* by Charles Dickens. That line drew you in and set the tone for the entire book.

The other two chapters you submit should be the ones

you believe are the most important or most interesting. If you have a dynamite closing chapter, include it. Don't worry about giving away the ending. Your goal is to sell your book.

Chapter Nine

THE QUERY LETTER

You may write for the joy of it, But the act of writing is not complete in itself. It has its end in its audience.

—Flannery O'Connor

he Query Letter is usually one page long and single-spaced. If you absolutely cannot include all of the following on one page, go to a second page. The margins must be at least one inch wide on the sides and three-quarters wide at the bottom.

A query letter is a greatly condensed version of a book proposal. If your book is nonfiction, it is always a good idea to write your book proposal and a few chapters before sending out query letters. Publishers of novels usually want to see the entire manuscript, not just a book proposal.

There are exceptions but they are rare. Preparing a proposal first will help you compose your query and, if an agent or publisher is interested in your idea and asks for more, you will be ready.

The information you will need to include in the query letter is virtually the same whether you are seeking an agent or a publisher. If you are sending the query directly to a publisher, simply change it accordingly. Instead of asking for representation, ask if they would be interested in publishing your book. Again, tailor your letter to the particular publisher you are contacting, being sure that they publish this kind of book.

When you write your query letter, imagine the literary agent or acquisitions editor who will be reading it and answer the following questions.

➢ **What do you want?** Explain your purpose for writing: you have a manuscript on (subject matter) and you are seeking representation or a publisher. The first paragraph should also include your "hook."

➢ **Why have you chosen this agency or publishing company?** Show that you have done your research by stating your reasons for choosing that particular agent: author recommendation, the agent's reputation, the agent represents similar works, etc. If you are sending this to a publisher, mention that they have published similar types of books.

➢ **What is your book about?** State the title and describe your book in a brief synopsis. This should not take up more than a few lines. Read book jackets and ads for ideas.

➢ **What is your background?** Explain your qualifications for writing this book. Are you an expert in this particular field? List other published works. If this is your first book, what else have you written? Television or film scripts? Magazine articles? Scientific papers?

➢ **What was your reason for writing this book?** Explain whether it is new information on the subject, a unique approach or an unusual story. Tell why you wanted to write it.

➢ **Who will want to read it?** Target your audience so that a publisher will know how to market your book. Research is imperative here.

➢ **What do you have to show me?** In your last paragraph explain what you would like to send. If you have written a nonfiction book, ask if you may send a book proposal; if it is a novel, offer to send a synopsis of it or the full manuscript.

Your query letter should be concise so choose your words carefully and check for spelling, grammatical construction, etc. This is the first example of your writing the agent or publisher will see, so make it the best it can be. Maintain a positive attitude about your creative work; don't be apologetic or defensive. And if you want a reply one way or the other, *always send a self-addressed stamped envelope.*

📖　📖　📖

On the following page is a query letter written by Patricia Fry, author of eight published books and innumerable magazine articles.

Natalie Chapman
MacMillan Books
1633 Broadway
New York, NY 10019

Dear Ms. Chapman:

Re: Book manuscript – *Fatherhood and Fathering:*
                  The Ultimate Guide For Today's Dad.

Fathering is finally fashionable. But because their role models
are outdated, countless men are struggling in this capacity. Today, fatherhood doesn't necessarily imply a wage-earning married man who lives with the mother of his children. The concept
of dear old dad has taken on new dimensions thus creating
greater challenges for men.

    The latest U.S. Census Bureau figures reveal that over 2.75
million children are in the custody of their fathers. The number
of primary care-taking fathers is on the rise as well. In 1991,
there were 1.4 million dads caring for their pre-school age children while their wives worked. And there's a sharp increase in
men involved in raising their stepchildren.

    At the other end of the spectrum are estranged dads who pay
child-support for the privilege of spending every other weekend
with their kids. Too many of these men become walk-away fathers, leaving children sadly and dangerously deficient in the
dad department.

    Although most of today's fathers desire more involvement
with their children, few know how to attain it. Working fathers
typically spend 10 minutes focusing on their children per day. In
a recent study, however, 74% of the men polled said they would
rather have a daddy-track job than a fast-track job: they want
jobs with fewer demands and flexible hours to allow more time
with their families.

    Fatherhood and Fathering is a book of information, educa-
tion, support, guidance and resources for every dad, with em-
phasis on the growing number of unconventional fathering

styles. It includes a fascinating history of fatherhood in this country and reports on the current trends representing fatherhood today, the struggles and obstacles fathers face and how fathers are coping in the '90s.

This extensively researched volume includes dozens of statistics depicting the state of and the effects of fatherhood as we know it today. There are over 100 individual stories and case histories to which the readers can relate and vital contributions from nearly 85 experts and professionals in the area of fatherhood and fatherlessness.

I have been writing for publication for 26 years. My articles have appeared in *The World and I, Los Angeles Times, Teaching Tolerance, Writer's Digest, Catholic Digest, Kiwanis Magazine, Living With Teens, Living With Children, Christian Parenting Today, L. A. Parent, Prime Times* and many others. I also have 7 books to my credit including *Creative Grandparenting Across the Miles: Ideas for Sharing Love, Faith and Family Traditions* (Liguori Publications, 1997).

Fatherhood and Fathering, The Ultimate Guide for Today's Dad is complete. I can send the manuscript or the book proposal. Let me know which you prefer.

Sincerely,
Patricia L. Fry

That is an excellent example. The author went to two pages but there were good reasons for it. I have even heard of four-page query letters that got the attention of a publishing company editor. But they are the exceptions to the rule.

Notice that Ms. Fry's book title describes exactly what the book is about. She does so again in the first paragraph. Her second paragraph shows the fruits of her research on marketability: "2.75 million children are in the custody of their fathers" and "In 1991 there were 1.4 million dads caring for their pre-school age children while their wives worked." Right away, you know this is a popular subject and likely to interest a lot of readers.

Her letter describes the challenges that divorced and separated fathers face in relating to their children, and the "walk-away" fathers who don't even try. When she says that children do not feel loved, she appeals to the emotions. Ms. Fry makes it clear that she has done extensive research and that she is a professional writer. This book would be hard for a publisher to resist.

Here are some examples to follow as you write your query letter.

THE FIRST PARAGRAPH

It's always a good idea to begin your letter with your "hook." Here are two examples:

> One of the most horrifying and baffling murder cases of the century began on a hot August night in Malibu with the brutal slaying of a beautiful porno star in the bedroom of noted TV evangelist Randy Saint. In *Saint and Sinner* I dissect the sloppy investigative work of the prosecution that put the wrong man on death row.

> Since ancient times, healers have told us our minds and bodies are one. Now, some amazing new research has proven this connection. A number of highly respected scientists and physicians have documented "miracle" cures using the power of the mind. This instant healing is something everyone can do and in my book, *If You Can Love, You Can Heal,* I explain how.

Make your opening paragraph as powerful as you can. Include the title of your book in this paragraph. This is the most important part of your letter so make sure it's a grabber.

THE BODY OF THE LETTER

Briefly synopsize your book. Include in the description of your book some of the more interesting passages, unknown facts, or your own involvement in the story, if pertinent. Here are two examples:

> Smoking is not the same addiction in women as it is in men. By the year 2000, women's death rate from smoking will surpass men's. This book addresses those differences and shows women how they can quit for good—without gaining weight. Because my own mother died prematurely from the effects of years of smoking, this book is dedicated to her.

> Born into wealth on a cotton plantation in the Old South sixteen years before the start of the Civil War, Susanna Campbell was given everything she could ever want except her parent's love. The delicate and beautiful girl was closer to her black nanny than she was to her own family. Still, no one could have predicted that Susanna would spend the Civil War years risking her life hiding runaway slaves. Her story is told through her recently unearthed journals buried nearly a century and a half ago.

Explain your reasons for writing the book and tell a little about yourself.

> As a physical therapist with a masters degree in psychology, I have found that the most valuable help for a child recovering from a serious accident is a therapeutic process I developed after my own devastating accident. Using this procedure, children get well in half the usual time.

Tell what the market for the book is and, in the last paragraph, describe what you would like to send. For help in writing the query letter go to your book proposal and highlight the most important points.

THE CLOSING PARAGRAPH

Describe what you would like to send. Your research may have indicated whether the agent or publisher would like to see the whole manuscript, a book proposal or a synopsis. If it is a book proposal, explain briefly what it consists of. Example:

> I would like to send you my book proposal along with three sample chapters, a total of 55 pages.

Chapter Ten

CONTRACTS

A verbal agreement isn't worth the paper it's written on.

—Attributed to Samuel Goldwyn

The following information should not be construed as legal advice, merely a discussion of what to expect in agreements you make with an agent or publisher and what to watch out for. Because laws and procedures are different in different states, countries and industries, and are subject to change, you are advised to get qualified legal advice before signing any agreement. Sometimes authors are so excited about finding an agent or a publisher that is interested in their book that they will sign just about anything. Remember the old saying, "Act in haste; repent at leisure," and proceed with caution.

This chapter is written in two parts.

PART I. THE LITERARY AGENCY AGREEMENT

In Chapter 7 the role of the agent was explained. Once you have found an agent who you think is the right one to represent you and your works, and that agent has offered representation, there are a number of questions you should ask. The Association of Authors' Representatives, Inc. (AAR) has a list of 22 topics they suggest you discuss. Until you know more about the agency, it is not advisable to sign any contract.

Find out if the agent is a member of the Association of Author's Representatives. All members must abide by a Canon of Ethics and satisfy the requirements for AAR membership which includes experience in the field. To qualify for membership the agent must have been "principally responsible for executed agreements concerning the grant of publication, translation or performance rights in ten different literary properties during the 18-month period preceding application." Here are some other questions to ask.

➢ How long has the agent/agency been in business and how many people are employed in the agency?

➢ Who in the agency will actually be handling my work?

➢ Will that person keep me apprised of the work the agency is doing on my behalf?

➢ Will you provide editorial input and career guidance?

➢ Do you provide submission lists and copies of publishers' rejection letters?

➤ Will you consult with me on all offers?

➤ What is your commission? (Most charge 15% for basic sales to U.S. publishers.)

➤ How do you process and disburse client funds?

➤ Do you charge for expenses incurred in handling my work such as postage, phone charges and copying costs and, if so, will you itemize such expenses for me?

➤ Do you issue annual 1099 tax forms?

➤ What do you expect of me as your client?

Taking the time to discuss those matters will help smooth the relationship with your agent. Before getting involved you must know what the agent's responsibility is and what yours is. One complaint agents make is that their clients expect them to be available to speak with them at all times. They also grumble that authors think agents aren't doing their job if they don't get them a deal with a publisher. But, the agents say, some manuscripts just aren't marketable for any number of reasons; and they have too many clients to talk to each one every day on the phone. They need time to contact publishers; that's in the best interest of the client.

Many writers say that after they signed the agreement with their agent they never heard from them again. The agent wouldn't even return their phone call.

Writers are often disappointed that their agent did not take an interest in their writing career.

Even if you feel that everything you wanted to know was addressed, other questions will come up during the course of your agent/author relationship, and maintaining clear and friendly lines of communication will make it easier on both of you.

For a small fee the AAR will furnish you a list of their members. Agents are listed according to their specialization: L = Literary; D = Dramatic; C = Children. They will not make recommendations to authors seeking representation, though.

Not all agents supply an agreement or contract for you to sign. Often the agent and author agree to terms informally. It's always a good idea to have the terms spelled out in a memo or letter from your agent. If the agent does not prepare an agreement, you can write one, based upon your understanding of the relationship, and send it to the agent asking if you are correct in your assumptions. That way there are likely to be fewer misunderstandings.

If you are offered a contract, discuss anything that is unclear to you with the agent and be sure that you understand it before you sign. Get as much information as you can before you sign any agreement with an agent (or anyone, for that matter). A good resource is *The Writer's Legal Companion: The Complete Handbook for the Working Writer* by Brad Bunnin and Peter Beren. It covers agency and publishing contracts, protecting your copyright, libel, taxes, and much more. The authors offer suggestions as to what issues should be covered in an agency contract. They go into these issues in greater detail in their book but here is a brief discussion of them.

The grant of authority

Set limits on your agent's authority to act in your behalf. You should have ultimate control over the sale of your rights. Agents should not sign a contract and bind you to it.

The agent's obligation

What will your agent do for you? This should be spelled out clearly. The agent should use her "best efforts" to sell your work and to act in "good faith" on your behalf. She should make a conscientious effort to sell your work. He should submit all offers to you, whether or not he thinks you should accept any of them. The agent should keep in touch with you and return your phone calls. You can't expect a busy, active agent to spend hours on the phone with you. But if you have not heard from him for a few months, it's reasonable to think he's forgotten you, and a call to him would be in order.

The deals you make and the contracts you sign are your own personal business and your agent should keep your financial affairs private and confidential. It is unethical for your agent to brag about the deal she got for you or the advance you received. Such loose talk could jeopardize future dealings with publishers.

Your agent should counsel and advise you, giving you the benefit of his experience. If she doesn't take the time to explain to you why you should or should not accept a particular offer, she isn't doing her job.

As the relationship between the agent and author can become an intensely personal one, you may want to be sure that the agency will not arbitrarily assign you to another agent in the future. Employees come and go and if the agent with whom you have established rapport leaves the agency, you may wish to terminate the agency relationship. Will they ask your permission before transferring you to someone else? This is a matter that should be clarified at the time you sign the agreement.

The author's obligation

Your obligation is to pay a commission when your agent sells your work. You may decide you want an "exclusive agency" relationship wherein you would not owe the agent a commission if you sold the work yourself. This might be the best kind of arrangement for you if you have extensive contacts within the publishing industry and have reason to believe that you could very well make a deal with a publisher on the golf course. (And probably more deals are made there than are made in offices.) Under this type of agreement, however, you must compensate your agent if *another* agent gets the deal for you. In that case, you would owe commissions to both agents.

Most agents want an "exclusive sale" agreement where you would be obligated to pay a commission no matter who sold your work. For most new authors that is probably okay. But beware of any arrangement where you end up selling your future.

Make sure your agent is representing you for a particular property or for specific works. In no case should you agree to letting him represent everything you have ever written or will write in the future.

Warranties

Both you and your agent need to warrant that you are free to enter the agreement, that you will be able to fully perform your obligation, and that you do not have any other contracts that will conflict with the provisions of the agency agreement.

Just as writers can tell horror stories about their agents, agents have some hair-raising tales about their clients. They've had clients who plagiarized someone else's work and represented it as their own, or who sold their work themselves without notifying them.

Commissions

Literary agents whose main client base consists of authors of books usually charge fifteen percent. Agents who represent film or television writers generally charge a ten percent commission. The Writers Guild of America (WGA) maintains a list of signatory agents who represent material such as screenplays, teleplays, stories, treatments, plot outlines, formats, breakdowns, sketches and narrations. Here is an excerpt from the WGA Agreement with Agents:

> The Guild disapproves of the practice followed by certain agencies of charging a "reading fee" or some similar fee to writers who submit literary material to them. Accordingly, the Guild will not be willing to list any such agency. The only monies listed agencies may collect from their clients is a 10% commission after successfully negotiating a deal.

As the author of a manuscript for a book, you would not ordinarily go to a WGA agent. Some exceptions might be if you have written a novel that would translate well onto the screen or a nonfiction book that could be made into a film or TV documentary. But even then, most experienced writers and agents will tell you that your best chance of getting it produced is to get it published as a book first.

As this is about getting your book completed and published, you will be seeking a literary agent who represents authors, not scriptwriters. There is no guild who tells those agents what they must charge. The fee is negotiable, however, and if you have extensive contacts and can help your agent get a publishing deal, you may be able to negotiate a ten percent commission. For foreign sales the commission ranges up to twenty percent. That is because the agent often has to split the commission with an agent in another country.

Your agent may also ask for an advance of about $100 for some out-of-pocket expenses such as postage, long-distance calling, and photocopying. That is not an unreasonable request and most agents will give you an accounting of how the money was spent.

The agency agreement usually provides for the publisher to pay your royalties directly to the agent who takes his percentage out and writes a check to you for the balance. As your agent will likely be able to read and understand a royalty statement better than you, that puts him in the position of monitoring the publisher.

Three things that should definitely be in the written agreement are (1) that your agent pays you your share promptly, (2) that you are allowed to examine the books at any time, and (3) that your money is kept in a client trust account, separate from the agency's own funds.

Multiple agents

As your agent may not be able to represent you for film and television sales, you may wish to sign with a WGA-approved agent, in addition to your literary agent. This may be a factor to include in the agreement, too.

The contract term

You may want to give your agent a definite amount of time to represent you. Usually one year is sufficient to find out whether the agent can sell your work, whether you are compatible, and whether you trust him enough to want to continue to work with him.

An agent may want more time because it may take many years before an author begins to earn significant income from her writing. If you still feel comfortable with your agent after a year, even if he hasn't made a deal, you may want to stay with him.

Terminating the agreement

You may not want to commit to a year or to any definite period of time. You may want the freedom to terminate the relationship at any time after giving a 30-day notice. Then if it doesn't seem to be working out, you can move on to another agent.

Some agency agreements contain post-termination clauses stating that they are owed a commission if you or another agent sells your work to a publisher within 90 days after termination of the agreement. If your agent has been working hard trying to sell your manuscript and has made a number of impressive contacts, that's a reasonable and fair request.

Learning more

Whenever possible, speak to an author the agent has represented and ask whether there were any problems before you sign an agreement for representation. The American Society of Journalists and Authors, the National Writers Association, and the National Writers Union maintain files on agents their members have worked with. The NWU has a Preferred Literary Agent Agreement and a pamphlet, "Understand the Author-Agent Relationship," that are available to members. If you are serious about your writing, it might be a good idea to join the NWU.

Whatever agreement you make with your agent, be sure that you both understand it completely and that the details are in writing.

PART II. THE PUBLISHING AGREEMENT

Many changes have taken place in the publishing world over the past few years which have made the publishing contract more complex than ever. As I am not a lawyer, I cannot give you legal advice, but I can alert you to some of the changes.

Technology is the major reason for the polymorphic publishing contract. The 20th century brought with it many new and different ways to record and transmit written works. Along with audiotape and videotape machines came radio, film and television. Following on the heels of photocopying machines were personal computers, scanners and printers. The computer made the Internet possible and that development made copyrighted material available to everyone on a massive scale. This explosion of new technologies has presented the enormous challenge of defining and protecting an author's rights to his/her literary creations.

Among the rights that must be spelled out in a publishing contract are paperback rights, book club rights, photocopying and facsimile rights, microfilm rights, audio rights, motion picture and television rights and the various categories of electronic rights which are evolving so fast as to defy legal definitions.

All of this makes a chapter on publishing contracts impossible to write in a comprehensive way. As media, technologies and markets change, a contract that works today is out of date tomorrow.

What you will see here is an overview to familiarize you with the kinds of agreements that have been used.

Before you sign any agreement with a publisher, be sure you know what you are signing. If you have an active, qualified agent with current contacts in the publishing field, she can help you understand the details of your contract. If you do not have an agent, it would be wise to get some legal advice from an attorney who specializes in, or at least is familiar with, publishing law. If neither of those options are available to you, get a recently published book that contains information on publishers' contracts. There are probably a number of good books on the subject but here are two that I can recommend. One is the book mentioned in Part I of this chapter: *The Writer's Legal Companion,* published in 1998. The other one is *Kirsch's Guide to the Book Contract,* published in 1999.

Both of those books have examples of publishing contracts in them. Kirsch's book discusses the various points in detail. However, don't expect to find a model contract that will cover every situation. As Kirsch says, "the book contract is a moving target." Each agreement must be fine-tuned to suit the author, the publisher, and the project.

Here are some things to look for in a book contract.

Grant of Rights

"**Primary Rights**" will include Hardcover, Trade Paperback, Mass-Market Paperback, Translation, Periodical Publication, Book Club, Photocopying and Facsimile, Microfilm, General Print Publication, Direct-Response Marketing, Sound Recordings, Electronic Books, Publishing-on-Demand, Database, Networks and On-Line Services, Interactive and Multimedia Rights.

Each of these items needs to be considered carefully and designed to fit your specific needs and wants. For example, if you had written a how-to book such as this, you might want to negotiate the right to sell your book at seminars you are presenting. In that case, you might purchase books from the publisher at a 50% discount and sell the books at full retail price. You may want to sell your books directly to the consumer, especially if you have an extensive mailing list of people who you know will be interested in your book.

"Secondary Rights" are Dramatic, Reading, Motion Picture and Television, Radio, Commercial, and Future Media and Technologies Rights. Those are called the "bundle of rights" that make up the most fundamental *deal points* in a book contract. "Deal points" as used here means the points considered essential to the parties making a book deal and include rights, territory, term, advance, and royalties.

"Electronic Rights" is a term that can have many meanings with the proliferation of new technologies. It is particularly challenging because things are changing too fast for settled legal definitions. There are no "standard" electronic rights clauses in publishing contracts. Be sure this is addressed in very specific language in your contract. It should be spelled out clearly who owns the right to exploit a book through a computer-based "publishing-on-demand" system, for example. Also called "print-on-demand," the computer is changing the way books are distributed and sold. In some areas the system is in place whereby a bookstore customer can order an "e-book" from a catalog. The book can then be printed out from an electronic database, bound, and delivered on the spot.

Author Compensation

"Advance Against Royalties" is money the author gets before the book is published. Often it is paid at the rate of one-third upon signing the agreement, one-third upon delivery of an acceptable manuscript, and one-third upon publication of the book. That money is not a no-strings gift from the publisher; it is deducted from future royalties on the sale of the book. Thus an author may not receive any royalty checks for a year or more.

How important is an advance? It depends on a number of factors. If an advance will allow you the freedom to work on your book instead of working a full-time job, it could be very important. Also, if you receive a significant advance, the publisher will want to protect its investment by advertising and promoting your book.

"Royalties on Publisher's Editions" is the share of sales the author receives. In the past this was often a percentage of the retail or cover price of the book. For example, if the price printed on the book cover was $10 and the author's royalty rate was 10%, the author received a dollar for each copy sold. A more frequent arrangement now is for the percentage to be based on the "invoice price" which is what the publisher receives from bookstores and wholesalers. Because a publisher may give them a discount of 40% or more, the publisher's net on a ten-dollar book might be six dollars, in which case the author would receive 60 cents per book.

The Manuscript

"Delivery of Manuscript" has to do with the date and form in which the author has agreed to deliver the completed manuscript. The publisher may ask for a computer disk containing the manuscript in a word-processing program and a hard copy (a printout).

"Artwork, Permissions, Index, and Other Materials" may include original art, illustrations, photos, charts, an index, bibliography, contents page, introduction, etc. It may also involve authorizations, permissions and endorsements.

"Publisher's Rights on Delivery" allows the publisher to terminate the agreement without further obligation to the author if the publisher finds the manuscript or any of the materials unacceptable. The publisher may give the author the opportunity to make revisions or corrections and resubmit. This clause also gives the publisher the right to terminate the agreement if the material is not delivered on time. In this case, the author will probably be required to repay the publisher for any advance she has received. The publisher may terminate the contract if changed conditions have adversely affected the salability of the work but, in that event, the author is usually allowed to keep the advance.

Publication

This section deals with authorizing the publisher to edit and revise the work, to design the book, set the price, print, advertise, and promote it, among other things. It may also state the date of publication, the number of free copies the author will receive and provide for revisions.

Copyright

This states that the publisher shall apply for a copyright in the name of the author and place the notice in the book. It also has to do with possible copyright infringement and how the parties may handle litigation.

Accounting

The publisher sets up a formal system of accounting where

it credits the author's account with royalties and any other payments and debits it for the advance, returned books, etc. This also states the author's audit rights.

Agency
The author authorizes and appoints the agent to act on behalf of the author to collect and receive payments and other communications from the publisher.

Warranties, Representations, and Indemnities
The author is asked to guarantee that his work will not result in a lawsuit and agrees to bear all costs of defending a claim if one is made. The author warrants that the work is not in public domain because, if anyone can freely publish it, the publisher doesn't have to acquire the rights from the author in the first place. The author also states that he is the sole proprietor of the work and has the authority to enter the agreement and grant the rights.

📖 📖 📖

NO AGENT? NO PUBLISHER? NO PROBLEM.

Well, maybe no problem. It depends on what your goals are. Many people have self-published, learning how to produce, promote, and market their books. As both author and publisher, those who choose to go this route could have a greater return on sales than they otherwise would have. Once you have completed the research for the Marketing Potential section of your book proposal, you should have a pretty good idea of where your book will sell.

Among my clients are authors who are producing a book with no plans to take it to a traditional publisher. They already know where and how to sell it. Some have already done so. One of these entrepreneurs is an English teacher who wrote a book about the various fields of writing with an explanation of what is involved in each one. He self-published it with a print run of 5,000 and sold out within a year or so, marketing it to home schooling programs.

Another self-publisher is a woman who writes a weekly column in the form of questions and answers on community associations for a major newspaper. She put her articles into a book and sold the book to homeowner, condominium and cooperative associations as well as to individuals who live in such communities. She is an authority on the subject and her book is always in demand. She sold all 12,000 copies of her first edition within two years and is preparing a second edition.

Patricia Fry has written several books. She has self-published some of them and has found publishers for others. Even after the expenses involved in editing, designing, printing, and promoting some of her self-published books, she has made a profit. *The Ojai Valley: an Illustrated History*, is in its second printing. Bookstores in Ojai, Ventura and other nearby cities in California stock and sell her books on a regular basis, not only to local residents but to tourists.

To learn more about what is involved in self-publishing, get Dan Poynter's *The Self-Publishing Manual: How to Write, Print and Sell Your Own Book.* You will find everything you need to know about becoming your own publisher in this book that many consider to be the "self-publishing bible." You may discover that publishing your own book is the best way for you to go.

Chapter Eleven

TEN WAYS TO PUBLISH YOUR BOOK

*Books, like men their authors, have no more than one way
of coming into the world, but there are ten thousand to go
out of it, and return no more.*

—Jonathan Swift, *A Tale of a Tub*

aybe in Swift's time there was only one way books came into the world, but that has changed. You, the author, have many choices now. There are more ways to publish your writing than ever before, with costs ranging from nothing to thousands of dollars. Here are a few of the ways to get your book published, with some pros and cons of each one.

1. FINDING A BOOK PUBLISHER
Advantages: Not only will it cost you nothing, you may get

an advance. The publisher will pay for printing, editing, promotion, distribution, etc. The perception is that it is more professional than a self-published book, although that perception is changing as the quality of self-published books improves.

Disadvantages: The author loses control. Royalties are much lower per book than the author's potential profit margin on a book he publishes himself. It will take 18 months to two years for the publisher to get the book out.

2. CO-PUBLISHING WITH AN ESTABLISHED PUBLISHER

Advantages: The publisher will know how to edit, promote and distribute the book. The costs of producing the book will be shared. The author will have the benefit of the publisher's professional advice.

Disadvantages: The author has less control than if he did it all himself. The author must share profits with the other publisher. There could be disagreements that are difficult to work out.

3. SELF-PUBLISHING A BOOK THE TRADITIONAL WAY

Advantages: The author has control of everything but the printing of the book. All profits belong to the author alone. Once it is finished and typeset, the author can get his book printed within one to two months. If the author has a niche market, he could make a greater profit than any other way.

Disadvantages: It can cost between $3,000 and $10,000 or more for printing alone. Unless the author can do it all himself, he must find qualified people to edit, create the cover and interior design and typeset the book. The author must do all the promotion, distribution and sales. Unless he has a ready market for it, he may never recover his initial costs to produce the book. He may also end up with several hundred or more unsold books.

4. SELF-PUBLISHING USING PRINT-ON-DEMAND

Advantages: Small numbers of the book can be printed costing $3 to $10 per book depending on the size, number of pages, and type of cover. The author could have 50 to 100 small paperbacks printed for a total cost of a few hundred dollars. She would not have storage problems for so few books. Additional books can be printed as needed. Time is another advantage. The book can be printed in a few days.

Disadvantages: As the technology is new there may be a problem with quality. Finding companies that do high-quality work on small print runs may be difficult. The cost per unit is usually higher than ordering from a regular printer.

5. SELF-PUBLISHING A SPIRAL-BOUND BOOK

Advantages: Photocopies can be made and books bound the same day by most photocopying companies. Or the author can purchase a binding machine and bind them herself as she needs them. She can also run off high-quality copies of the pages on her own printer.

Disadvantages: It can end up costing more than print-on-demand and does not look as professional. Spiral-bound books have no spine on which to put the title of the book and because of that, many book stores and libraries will not carry it. There are spiral-bound books where the cover is folded so that there is a spine; however, that process may not be available from a local photocopying company nor to an individual using a spiral binding machine.

6. CREATING A HAND-CRAFTED BOOK

Advantages: It may be appropriate for art books, poetry, or family history, and it becomes a work of art in itself. It is a great creative outlet for authors who are also artists or craftsmen and who enjoy the process of creating the entire product. The author has total control. If the author chooses not to bind it himself, he can have it handbound for $6 to $10 per book cover.

Disadvantages: Depending upon the materials used, it could be quite costly per unit. Only limited numbers of books could be produced this way. Handcrafting a book is a time-consuming process.

7. PUBLISHING AS E-MAIL ON THE INTERNET

Advantages: It can be done without incurring any printing costs. It can reach a wide market.

Disadvantages: The author would have to figure out how to sell his book to the reader. He would have to learn what it takes to reach a wide market.

8. PRODUCING A BOOK ON A FLOPPY DISK OR CD

Advantages: Copies can be made relatively inexpensively by the author. Disks and CDs are less bulky to carry than a printed book. They can be read on a computer screen or printed out.

Disadvantages: It must be read on a computer or printed out. It is too easily copied. It would be hard to get bookstores to carry it.

9. PRODUCING AS AN AUDIOBOOK

Advantages: Cost, depending on whether author has to pay

for a recording studio or records it himself. It can be "read" by the blind or listened to on long automobile trips. It can be produced in the author's own voice. It could be valuable for family histories and memoirs. It could later be transcribed and made into a printed book.

Disadvantage: Promotion and distribution would be challenging. If the author doesn't have a pleasant voice that records well, she may have to hire a professional actor.

10. PUBLISHING AS AN E-BOOK (ELECTRONIC BOOK)

This format is the most interesting one of all if you want to keep your costs down and become involved in an exciting new technology in book publishing.

Stephen King offered his recent 66-page short story, *Riding the Bullet,* exclusively on the Internet. Published by Simon & Schuster Online, it is available as an e-book that buyers can download for $2.50.

To explain the electronic book concept I asked Virginia Lawrence, an expert in the field, for permission to reprint an article on this subject that she wrote for *SPAWNews,* the newsletter of Small Publishers, Artists & Writers Network (SPAWN). Her article addresses both the advantages and disadvantages.

THE E-BOOK
AN IMPORTANT NEW DIRECTION IN PUBLISHING?

by Virginia Lawrence, Ph.D.

As artists, writers, and publishers using the Internet, we have all heard about e-books, yet there seems to be little e-book awareness in the popular press. Why? There are several reasons: no major player has caught the fancy of general-interest editorial staff, the methods used to create and deliver e-books are still in flux, and the questions of appropriate royalties and pricing remain open.

E-BOOK FORMAT

E-books available today range from simple text files to html files to Adobe pdf files to full-fledged multimedia extravaganzas. Some e-books are meant only for viewing on a full-size computer monitor, while others are built for printing, and others are formatted especially for the Rocket Book or the Palm Pilot.

E-BOOK DELIVERY

Consider e-book delivery systems: E-books can be sold on CDs or even floppies, so those delivery systems are reasonably straightforward for people who are somewhat familiar with a computer. E-books can also be sold in downloadable files. As long as a downloadable purchase process is streamlined and carefully explained, downloadable delivery can be a boon to both the purchaser and the publisher.

E-BOOK ROYALTIES AND PRICES

At last report, the major print publishers were offering the usual print royalties or even less in royalty to authors who agreed to be published in e-book format. At the same time, those publishers were charging hard-cover prices for e-books. This seems unnecessarily greedy, doesn't it?

E-BOOK COSTS VERSUS HARDCOVER COSTS

An e-book delivered online as a file will require editing and formatting, but it will not require an expensive print run or storage of the resulting books. An e-book delivered online doesn't even have any shipping costs after the delivery system has been set up.

Of course, an e-book on a CD does involve duplication costs, but those are lower than hard-cover printing, and CD storage takes no more than one quarter the space required for book storage. Shipping costs for feather-light CDs are lower than for hardcover books.

The price of an e-book should reflect the publisher's lower costs. As word spreads in the popular media that e-books are available at reasonable prices, and e-books are available for immediate gratification by download, the real e-book groundswell will begin.

Virginia Lawrence is SPAWN's Webmaster. She is an Information Architect who publishes both in print and online. Her Web site is <http://www.cognitext.com.

Now you have much of the information you need to produce a book. You may need to do more research and you may need to get help for some parts of the process but it should no longer be a mystery to you. I wish you joy in your creative adventure into authorship.

Chapter Twelve

ASSEMBLE YOUR TOOLS

Give us the tools and we will finish the job.
—Winston Churchill,
Radio Broadcast, February 9, 1941

*Y*ou may feel that the only tools you need to write a book are a pen and a pad of paper. And that may be so. But if you want to be accurate and informed, you will need books for research. If you want to be able to write and edit quickly, you will need a word processor or a computer. If you want to send your manuscript out it must be printed, so you will need a printer attached to your computer.

In the 1800s, Thomas Carlyle said, "Man is a tool-using animal. . . . Without tools he is nothing, with tools he is all." He may not have been referring to writers but he could have been. Because without some basic tools, your book remains an idea in your head, incomplete, unrealized, unrecorded.

At any stage in your writing you can assemble your tools, but the best time to start getting them together is before you begin the job. Think of how it would be if the only planning you did to paint your living room was to buy the paint and the paintbrush. You would soon find that you needed tools to open the paint can and to stir the paint with. After you started painting you'd discover that you needed a drop cloth so that you wouldn't ruin the floor. And you might have to stop and spackle the nail holes before you continued. Planning ahead and assembling all the tools you needed would have helped the process move along more smoothly. The same is true for writing.

Here's a list of some tools to consider getting, with a box for you to check off each one as you acquire it. Some you may not need or want or be able to get right now, and some you will already have.

EQUIPMENT

☐ a computer (and monitor), word processor or electric typewriter (preferably a correcting one)

☐ a laser or inkjet printer

☐ a desk, tabletop or flat area that is for your exclusive use

☐ a good, supportive and comfortable chair on casters so you can move it around easily

☐ a file cabinet or portable file box so you can keep your rough drafts, notes, and research information in order

☐ a telephone

☐ a fax

☐ a scanner

☐ good lighting

BOOKS

☐ an unabridged dictionary, the latest edition

☐ a desk dictionary, the most recent available

☐ a thesaurus

☐ a book of quotations such as *Bartlett's Familiar Quotations* or *The Oxford Dictionary of Quotations*

☐ an encyclopedia, either in print or on a computer disk, the most recent available

☐ *The Chicago Manual of Style*

☐ this year's edition of *Writer's Market*

☐ any other reference books that will be of help in your particular writing project

OFFICE SUPPLIES

☐ paper: notepads and typing/computer paper

☐ red pens to mark corrections and changes on your printed pages

☐ black or blue pens for jotting down notes

☐ yellow highlighter pens

☐ an extra ink cartridge for your printer

☐ computer disks to save your work on

You may think of more things you should have on hand such as scissors, paperclips, cellophane tape, and so forth. Make a list of all the tools you think you will need and get them before you start writing. Not only will it save you time in the future, it will put you in the right frame of mind to write and could assuage that bad habit of most writers: procrastination.

That blockbuster novel may be germinating inside your brain at this very moment. You just could be a creative genius. You might have enormous talent—far more than anyone would guess. But to get your ideas down on paper in a presentable form you will have to be more than an accomplished author—you must also be a good craftsman. You still need the tools of the trade. They are of the utmost importance in your ability to finish the job.

YOUR TIME

You need to not only gather your tools and set up your work space, you need to organize your time so that you can spend an hour or more each day writing. Once you get going, you may find that you are just getting warmed up in an hour. Then you may want to change your daily schedule or even your life style so that you can fit in a three-hour writing period each day.

It takes dedication and perseverance to write a book. How you prepare yourself depends on whether you are a serious writer or a hobbyist. Which one are you?

Resources

PUBLICATIONS

The American Directory of Writer's Guidelines: What Editors Want, What Editors Buy compiled and edited by John C. Mutchler; Quill Driver Books

Bird by Bird: Some Instructions on Writing and Life, by Anne Lamott, Anchor Books/Doubleday

Books in Print and *Forthcoming Books,* published by R.R. Bowker & Co.

The Cambridge Factfinder, published by Cambridge University Press

The Chicago Manual of Style, The University of Chicago Press

The Copyright Permission and Libel Handbook: A Step-by-Step Guide for Writers, Editors, and Publishers, by Lloyd J. Jassin and Steven C. Schechter; John Wiley & Sons, Inc. 1998. 198 pages.

Editing, Fact and Fiction: A Concise Guide to Book Editing, by Leslie T. Sharpe and Irene Gunther, Cambridge University Press

The Fisher Report, Prof. Jim Fisher, Edinboro University, Dept. of Political Science and Criminal Justice, Hendricks

Hall, Edinboro, PA 16444. This contains a "rogues gallery" of disreputable and dishonest agents.

Guide to Literary Agents, Writer's Digest Books. Published annually.

How to Get Happily Published: A Complete and Candid Guide (Fifth Edition) by Judith Appelbaum; published by Harper Perennial

How to Market You and Your Book by Richard F.X. O'Connor; published by O'Connor House

How to Write a Book Proposal by Michael Larsen; Writer's Digest Books

The Insider's Guide to Book Editors, Publishers & Literary Agents, by Jeff Herman, published by Prima Communications

Jump Start Your Book Sales: A Money-Making Guide for Authors, Independent Publishers and Small Presses, by Marilyn & Tom Ross, Communication Creativity, P.O. Box 909, Buena Vista, CO 81211

Kirsch's Guide to the Book Contract: for Authors, Publishers, Editors and Agents, by Jonathan Kirsch, published by Acrobat Books

Kirsch's Handbook of Publishing Law: for Authors, Publishers, Editors and Agents, by Jonathan Kirsch, published by Acrobat Books

Literary Agents: A Writer's Guide, published by Poets & Writers

Literary Agents of North America, by Arthur Orrmont, published by Author Aid & Research Assoc. International. 340 E. 52nd Street, New York, NY 10022; phone (212) 758-4213. Listings of over 650 agents, their interests and charges

Literary Market Place, R.R. Bowker, A Reed Reference Publishing Co. Published annually.

Merriam-Webster's Manual for Writers & Editors: A clear, authoritative guide to effective writing and publishing, from the editors of *Merriam-Webster's Collegiate Dictionary*

On Writing Well: The Classic Guide to Writing Nonfiction, by William Zinsser, HarperPerennial

The Portable Writers' Conference: Your Guide to Getting and Staying Published, Edited by Stephen Blake Mettee, Quill Driver Books. (To order, call 1-800-497-4909)

Publishers Weekly (The International News Magazine of Book Publishing and Bookselling) A Cahners/R.R. Bowker Publication

The Self-Publishing Manual: How to Write, Print and Sell Your Own Book, by Dan Poynter; Para Publishing, P.O. Box 8206, Santa Barbara, CA 93118-8206

Write & Grow Rich: Using Speech Recognition to Dictate Your How-to Book, by Dan Poynter, Para Publishing

The Writer, monthly magazine, $28, 120 Boylston Street, Boston, MA 02116

Writer's Digest, monthly magazine, $27, 1507 Dana Avenue, Cincinnati, OH 45207

Writer's Guide to Hollywood Producers, Directors and Screenwriter's Agents, by Skip Press, Prima Publishing, 3875 Atherton Road, Rocklin, CA 95765-3716; phone (916) 632-4400.

The Writer's Handbook, (110 Chapters on How to Write; 3200 Markets for Manuscripts) edited by Sylvia K. Burack; published by The Writer Inc. Published annually

Writer's Market, Where & How to Sell What You Write, Writer's Digest Books. Published annually.

Write the Perfect Book Proposal; 10 Proposals that Sold and Why, by Jeff Herman and Deborah M. Adams; published by John Wiley & Sons, Inc.

Writing Nonfiction; Turning Thoughts into Books, by Dan Poynter; Para Publishing, P.O. Box 8206, Santa Barbara, CA 93118-8206

ORGANIZATIONS

Agent Research & Evaluation, 334 E. 30th Street, New York, NY 10016. AR&E tracks agents in court records and the press. They publish a newsletter and sell reports from their database

American Society of Journalists & Authors, Inc., 1501 Broadway, Suite 302, New York, NY 10036. Dues are $165/year. Phone: (212) 997-0947; Fax 768-7414; e-mail 75227.1650@compuserve.com

Association of Authors' Representatives (AAR), 3rd floor, 10 Astor Place, New York, NY 10003. (212) 353-3709. Literary agents who are members of AAR subscribe to a code of ethics. Send $7 and SAE with 55 cents for postage for a list of member agents

The Authors Guild, 330 W. 42nd Street, New York, NY 10036. (212) 563-5904; fax (212) 564-8363. Provides a variety of services including a quarterly newsletter, a guide to publishing contracts, and health insurance. Dues are $90/year and include membership in The Authors League of America

The Authors League of America, 330 W. 42nd Street, New York, NY 10036. (212) 564-8350. A sister organization to The Authors Guild

Independent Literary Agents Association (ILAA), 55 Fifth Avenue, New York, NY 10003. Ask for a list of their members

National Writers Union, East Coast Office: 113 University Place, 6th floor New York, NY 10003. (212) 254-0279; fax (212) 254-0673

National Writers Union, West Coast Office: 337 W. 17th Street, Suite 101, Oakland, CA 94612. (510) 839-0110; fax (510) 839-6097. E-mail: nwu@nwu.org. Web site: http://www.nwu.org/nwu/. A trade union committed to improving the working conditions of freelance writers. Dues based on writing income start at $90/year

PEN American Center, 568 Broadway, New York, NY 10012. (212) 334-1660; fax (212) 334-2181. The largest of 124 centers worldwide. Membership consists of playwrights, essayists, editors and novelists.

Science Fiction & Fantasy Writers of America, Inc., 532 La Guardia Place #632, New York, NY 10012-1428. They have a tutorial of what to look for in an agent, a model agent contract, case studies and a list of resources

Small Publishers, Artists & Writers Network (SPAWN) P.O. Box 2653, Ventura, CA 93002-2653; Phone/fax: (805) 643-2403. Web site: www.spawn.org. A nonprofit organization formed to "provide education, information, resources and a supportive networking environment for artists, writers, and other creative people interested in the publishing process."

Writers Guild of America-East, 555 W. 57th St., New York, NY 10019. (212) 767-7800; fax (212) 582-1909. A labor union representing professional writers in motion pictures, television and radio. Members must be published or employed in the field.

Writers Guild of America-West, 8955 Beverly Blvd.,
West Hollywood, CA 90048. (213) 550-1000. Web site:
http://www.wga.org. Provides a list of WGA signatory
agents for $2 and SASE sent to Agency Department. Both
WGAE and WGAW provide a registration service for literary material.

NOTE:
The above lists of resources are only a few available to
authors. There are many valuable publications and organizations that offer specific help. Your goals, needs, specialty
and location will determine which ones are right for you.